Appalachian Granny

Magick and Musings of an Appalachian Witch

Appalachia, in fact, is a very matriarchal culture. We revere our grandmothers and mothers.

In Appalachia, everyone has a fierce granny story.

Anthony Harkins, author

I grew up down in the hills of Virginia. I can be in Kentucky in 20 minutes, Tennessee in 20 minutes, or in the state of West Virginia in 20 minutes. And, it's down in the Appalachian Mountains, down there. And, it's sort of a poorer country. Most of the livelihood is coal mining and logging, working in the woods and things like that. Most people has a hard life down that way.

Dr. Ralph Stanley, musician

When they lie my body in the green, green grass, I will whisper quiet secrets to the animals that pass, about the times I swore I was never coming back. . .but, I lied. I am Appalachia.

Josiah Leming, musician

Dedicated to the ancestors: Great-great granny Sarah Sally Fletcher, Great-granny Nannie Crouse Roberts, Granny Lennie Lewis Roberts, Mom Alice Roberts, and to those who came before.

And, to the future, our little Anna, Klaven, Kaden, and Alice Ephraim, Shiloh, Thaddeus, Aidan and Finn.

THERE'S A LITTLE

WITCH

IN ALL OF US

Thank you to my husband, Kenneth O'Keefe, for his patience. Writing can make your partner a book widower, or so I've heard.

Appalachian Granny Witch Magick

Magick and Musings of an Appalachian Mountain Witch

Reaper Publishing, LLC
Fleetwood, NC

ISBN-13: 978-1-951583-09-5   Reaper Publishing, LLC

Printed in the United States of America.

Appalachian Granny Witch Magick

Magick and Musings of an Appalachian Mountain Witch

The Mountains are calling and I must go.

- John Muir-

Table of Contents

Chapters

There's Magick in Them Mountains

When I was small
Living amongst the Appalachian Mountains,
My grandma pointed into the distance one day
And said, "You know, there's magick in them mountains."

Her words reverberate through the tunnel of time,
Reminding me that life is short, the mountains old.
These monoliths of rock, and dirt, and greenery,
Will be here eons after my descendants are born, and I am gone.

That image gives me comfort,
To know the mountains, where I live
Will remain unchanged for those whom I would love,
If only I were there.

Within the hollers of this mystical land,
Overshadowed by the all-seeing, all-knowing mountains,
Lies a magick that few know about and to which fewer connect.
A magick of rare power, proving granny right,
There's magick in these Appalachian Mountains.

Pat Bussard O'Keefe

A Warning

This book is not recommended for children. The herbs and other items that are found within a spell shared in this book could be things to which you, or someone else may have an allergy or sensitivity.

The author and publisher strongly advise against using any spells containing herbs and other items that could cause severe reactions. **Always know if you have allergies to something before you use it in a spell.** Also, if an herb is known to be poisonous, be very careful in how you handle that botanical. Do your research! If something in a spell is unknown to you, look it up to make sure it is not noxious.

Anyone who uses the spells in this book to cast spellwork does so entirely at their own risk and the author and publisher accepts no liability if the spells do not manifest as hoped or if they manifest in a negative sense.

*Magick is spelled with a "k" in this book to differentiate real magick from stage magic.

Chapter 1

A Word About the Author and Granny Witches

VICK'S FLOWER Vegetable Garden

gentle art ... lies her
... and in thy soul ... ... and
... and thy heart is filled with ...
... joys that brighten with ... touch of ... fancy.

To thee, the high broadway of life, ... stretcheth
to the grave and endeth in Eternity, ...
and a thousand forms of varied ... ...
surface. Lofty and ... sentiment, and
thy ... forth in a ... ...
innocent ... in thee, ...
spirits. ... ... about to
go forth into the mighty world, ... may
circle thee about, or rude adversity ... thy ... its
chilly hand. That it may not ... thy gentle
soul to ... its generous sympathies — to ... sufferings
of joy, and sicken it of earth's bright ... is the prayer
of her who never uttered one more ... and holy than
she now murmurs for thy happiness.

*T*he Appalachian Mountains are the home of granny witches, also known as granny women, wise women, or cunning folk. Although mountain magick was practiced by some men, many women were the healers and mystics of their family clans, thus the name, "Granny Witches." These women and men came from the hollers of mountains so high and valleys so narrow in some places that it shadowed the landscape. For some of these folks, this lack of sunshine reaching the ground in their holler (narrow valley) made evening come to their "neck of the woods," sooner than it did for their neighbors across the mountain.

Some of the oldest parts of the Appalachian Mountains are more than one billion years old (Randolph). These ancient natural structures have seen the decline and extinction of the dinosaurs and the rise and proliferation of man. Always silently observing, these mountains conceal the power of natural magick. A magick revealed to those whose ancestors' blood, sweat, and tears nourished the mountains they called home. For only a few who have moved here from other places, Appalachia has revealed her secrets, whispering them to the new initiate.

Pat Bussard O'Keefe is an eclectic mountain witch whose spells and philosophy of magick are revealed in <u>Appalachian Granny Witch Magick</u>. She is a direct descendant of the original granny women of the Appalachian region. These are her musings about a number of things Appalachian-related. Other folks may have different opinions on these topics. That's ok, too. If you are interested, you can read in-depth about her family background in the book, <u>Spells and Stories of The Sisterhood of Magick and Wonders,</u> (O'Keefe, et al).

Although she uses Appalachian magick learned through her (primarily) female ancestors, she has developed her own style over time. Pat's primary tool as an energy witch, is drawing and utilizing Divine energy to manifest reality. She has selected over 50 of her most successful spells for this book. Some of those spells were handed down directly from her forebears, some were developed as she walked her own spiritual journey. Either way, the spells within this book were created by women who are connected with mountain magick.

Her bloodline runs deep through the southern Appalachian mountains, as thick as the coal beds that pepper these hills, and as dense as the trees from which Pat's granddad made his living as a logger, or as lush as the farm on which her daughter now lives. She has grown up with the siren song of the mountains, mysterious and mystical. Like her ancestors, the granny women, she has natural psychic and energy healing abilities.

There were no doctors and no chemical pharmaceuticals in those mountains during her great-granny's time. It gave them the opportunity to learn how to heal from the botanicals and energy that were available to them.

Although Pat is trained as a Reiki Master, Appalachian root energy is the foundation for the energy healing she does. The gifts of second sight she has are also a gift from her ancestral grannies.

Sit for a spell with Pat to learn magick and hear stories from a latter-day Appalachian Mountain granny.

The unique thing about Appalachian folk magic is that there's no one right way to do it. Depending on what mountain or holler your family is from, you might practice differently. These differences are due, in part, to the close clans of the Irish and Scottish who came here. Maybe those traditions were unique to the clan and the region they came from. These were further separated by oral traditions being passed down through generations in different regions and evolving over time, (Richards, 2019).

Jake Richards
Backwoods Witchcraft

Chapter 2

Growing up in the Mountains

Appalachian mountain life could be hard at times. But, when I was growing up, there was always food in the pantry because my mom and granny put it there through hard work in the garden.

I also had a roof over my head, thanks to my grandpaw and granny. They had built the little tarpaper house we lived in with their own hands. Some of the materials they used to build the house were cannibalized from what was known locally as the Sam Hannah Holler House. This house was known in the area for being haunted.

My mother had an experience there when she was little. Her parents were visiting with the relatives who lived there at the time, and she was asked to go up the stairs to the second floor landing. She encountered both a ghostly woman who disappeared when she walked around a corner and a little spirit boy who rolled a ball back to her, several times. You can read about those stories in detail in Thirty True Tales of the Weird, Unusual and Macabre, (Bussard, 2013).

"Ghosts dwelled in the Old Sam Hannah 'Holler' house," so claimed my mother and others of her generation and geographical location. My grandmother swore that about the same time Point Pleasant was experiencing its unpleasant encounter with what would become known as the "Mothman," that a giant bird/man like creature was seen in her region of West Virginia. The story of the mystery cryptid that once dwelled at the old TNT plant in Point Pleasant has survived and a festival now celebrates its time among the town's residents.

The story about the haunted Hannah house is beginning to fade as those who had contact with the ghosts that dwelled in that house die and take their memories with them. . . Below are related my mother's experiences in the house, lest they be lost in the sandstorm of time.

The Old Sam Hannah house was a large, clapboard home. The structure visually struck those who saw it as literally rising up from the ground to tower over the viewer. The house was constructed in the middle of nowhere in the Spring Creek area of West Virginia and many who entered it often met with more than the living residents of the home. The dead walked the halls of the old house, seemingly eager to make an impression on its' unlucky guests.

My mother, Alice Roberts, was a young girl when she often visited relatives living in the Hannah house. It was already an old house then, but well kept. The freshly painted white clapboard made the house stand out from the explosion of green that Mother Nature kindly provided. She and her sister and brothers would often sit on the front porch and survey the world. Sometimes, she and her siblings were relegated to the much darker interior of the house. My mother would describe the feeling of oppression that would overcome them when they entered the house. The light, she would say, found it difficult to force its way deeply into the core of the home, instead giving up and remaining near the windows and doors.

In addition to the spirits of the woman and young boy that my mother accidently met on the landing of that old house, she also had another ghostly experience at that location. An experience which was shared with her mother and little brother. This story was found amongst others in a book of writings that my mother left behind after she transitioned into the otherworld.

She had some psychic experiences in the Hannah house when she was a visitor, when her uncle and aunt lived there. At one time, however, she and her family also resided in the locally famous haunted house.

'When we lived in the old Sam Hannah House, mom had to keep me with her when she did the chores, including milking the cows and laying in wood, and had to leave six-month-old little brother Van in the baby bed.

"One night, mom was reading and suddenly she picked up Van and grabbed my hand and down that holler we went. Mom was scared, I didn't know why, but I was terrified.

"We met dad coming up the holler and went back home. Only later did I find out about all the people who had seen or heard things there. It was several years later, when I had my own experiences there.

"I asked mom later on what had scared her into leaving the house. She said she didn't know but had an overwhelming feeling that she needed to get us kids out.

"It was really the nicest house we ever lived in. It had three real old stone fireplaces. The walls were warm chestnut. It had four bedrooms, a large dining room, kitchen, a pantry under the stairs, and a room at the top of the stairs that was used as a closet and storage place. It was called the Sam Hannah house because of who built it," (Roberts, 2003).

I don't know if they brought something home with them from the Hannah house when they built the little house in the valley from some of its parts, or if it was because an artesian spring ran directly under the house, which is known to be a catalyst for ghostly activity, or both. But the house I grew up in had more activity and more unusual activity (by paranormal investigative standards) than any other location I have ever personally visited. It even had a room, that while I lived in the house, had a large 1930s chifforobe, a bed, a side table and a large, heavy vanity with a humongous round, moonlike mirror. When I went back to the house years later to visit my uncle who now lived in the house, I was shocked. The only thing that could fit in that room was a bed, small table, and small chest of drawers. There are simply too many stories to tell about that little house in the valley, at the foot of Pocahontas mountain in West Virginia.

My two sisters, Tracey and Pam, and our mom were sitting on the couch one day when we heard a huge explosion coming from the kitchen. When we ran into the room, we saw that the butcher knife had flown from the counter and had landed with enough force to be sticking straight up from the floor in the geographic center of the kitchen. In addition, all over the knife and the floor, was a red liquid, splattered everywhere.

Rosemary Ellen Guiley, the well-known writer and researcher whom I respected immensely, once told me that she felt that there was so much activity in West Virginia and Ohio because of the convergence of the powerful lines of the Earth's power grid, known as ley lines.

There is something special about West Virginia. There's an energy there that you need to experience to really understand how powerful this area is.

I knew I was poor growing up, because I didn't have the clothes that a lot of the other kids wore to school. But school was the only place that I felt poor. At home, I always felt I had enough. That is a really good feeling for a kid. And, I had something that I realize now is pretty special, a love for reading.

Granny was an avid reader and whatever she read, I read. I was a pretty insatiable reader when I was growing up, because there wasn't anything else to do! We got one television channel because granddad ran an antenna up on the mountain, years before he died in a car crash. By today's standards, one channel of visual entertainment could be considered to be child cruelty.

And, to put insult on that cake, if I wanted to watch TV, I was either watching Lawrence Welk or a cowboy movie. Neither were too interesting for a girl growing up. Although I did end up reading every western Louis L'Amour ever wrote, because granny read them and because they were basically romance novels.

But, granny wasn't just reading westerns, she was reading books with titles like, Wonders of the World, Chariots of the Gods, by Erich Von Daniken, The Dark Arts, by Richard Cavendish, and so many other tomes of esoteric knowledge. She was also a faithful subscriber to the famously forward-thinking *Fate Magazine*. Again, I was the happy recipient of the magazine, as soon as she was done reading the publication.

Granny had a special fascination with the famous psychic and astrologer Jeane Dixon, so I was hearing and reading about her, too. Dixon is the psychic who was given credit for telling President John F. Kennedy to avoid going to Dallas, Texas. We all know now what the President's fateful trip to that city cost the nation and the Kennedy family. I have a signed, first edition copy of her biography, <u>Jeane Dixon, My Life and Prophecies.</u>

Did Dixon accurately predict the assassination of the president? Some say yes, and others say they have definitive proof she didn't. I like to think that she did, because my granny admired her so much.

My mother, however, was fascinated by Sybil Leek. Born in 1917, Leek was a well-known witch, one of the first to pop out of the broom closet after the repeal in 1951 of Britain's Witchcraft Act of 1735. The 200-year-old Witchcraft Act was replaced at that time with the Fraudulent Mediums Act, (Wikipedia contributors, 2023.)

Yes, witches were freed (figuratively speaking), but fake mediums needed to beware the ramifications of their charlatanry. Why? Because the Spiritualist community had a very good lobbying effort going on at the time. Spiritualists believe in Christian tenents, they also believe that a true medium can talk with the dead. I must say, I definitely have that in common with Spiritualists. Leek, herself, was well-known as a psychic medium, frequently working with the godfather of parapsychology himself, Dr. Hans Holzer, on paranormal investigations. Although, there were many other witches with whom she quarreled and some who thought she was less than talented, she is still a highly interesting person.

Like some better-known psychics, my mother read palms and my granny read the spirit board and read tea or coffee grounds. However, the board was her favorite psychic tool.

For the area we lived in, this was considered very unusual. My family was like an Appalachian version of the Addams Family, but without any of its male members amongst the primary cast.

I remember being around 14 years old and walking to a graveyard about a half mile away from my house to read, while sitting on a branch up in a tree. One day, while reading, I noticed a man in the back of the graveyard. He had dark hair and was wearing a tan trench coat. I knew he was a spirit, and I wasn't too concerned, because he was so far back from where I sat in the graveyard's tree.

A few minutes later, I looked up and he was closer to me, while his eyes were locked directly on me. I remember noticing how dark his eyes were and I became very, very afraid. I jumped down as fast as I could, while running towards the old gate of the cemetery fence and shouted, "You cannot follow me," as I skedaddled out of that place. I never saw the spirit of that man again, if that is what he was. Nor, did I want to cross paths with him at a later date.

Growing up in the mountains was a wonderful experience. Growing up psychic and coming from a family with very different interests that most other people didn't share in our region, made us stand out. And, of course, that brings its own issues.

Years have passed now and so many things have happened along the way that have shaped who I have become as a person and a spiritual being.

The backdrop for the journey of my life was and continues to be the Appalachian Mountains and that is truly a blessing.

Chapter 3

Granny Witches

A granny witch was someone who took care of her family the best way she knew how, and she took care of folks in her community, too, when she could. These women would have never said that they were witches; that's what others might say about them. You could find most of them at church on Sunday.

It didn't keep them from talking about the preacher, though, especially if they felt there was too much fire and brimstone in his sermon or not enough. Granny women were spiritual through and through. So spiritual was she that my little great-granny Nannie (how my mom spelled her name) Crouse Roberts, who never got the chance to go to school to get some "learnin," wanted to read the Bible. She wanted this so badly that she prayed a lot on the subject. "God, if you'll just let me read, I promise you, the only thing I will ever read is the Good Book."

She liked her preacher, but she wanted to read the words that the preacher was saying to the congregation herself. Great Granny was a mighty powerful spiritual being. One day she woke up and she could read! From that day forward, she only read the Bible, every day for the rest of her life.

Now, great-granddaddy Lone Roberts, (he was called 'Pap' by my mom and other members of his family), he got kind of a raw deal out of her zealous attention to the fact that she would only read the Good Book. Pap got an education to the third grade, which meant he could read. Great granny was a girl in the mountains and in those days, many never got to set foot in a classroom. It was thought they didn't need any education. The mountain way of thinking at that time was, why educate someone whose future was exclusively being and wife and a mother?

Pap noticed that his "westerns," as he called his cowboy books, were going missing. One day, he caught great granny tossing one in the garbage. He was upset, because books were scarce in the mountains in those days. "Doggone it, Nannie, you made that deal with God; I didn't," he exclaimed!

Great granny was what they called a "wart witch." She could whisper a wart off of you in no time flat. When I was a little girl, I got a really large wart on my hand. I remember my great-granny holding my hand and placing a chicken bone on the wart. She put her lips close to the hand and she started whispering in a very low voice. When she finished, she raised her head, looked at me, and said, "Pat, in two weeks that ol' wart will fall off." I remember the confidence she had in her words. Sure enough, two weeks later the wart fell off.

She wasn't alone; there were other wart witches in the mountains of Appalachia. They helped a lot of people like me rid themselves of warts. But they did a whole lot more than that.

These women, along with their male counterparts, were the herbalists and healers of the mountains. There were no doctors; you might ride for miles just to get to a little town with few inhabitants. In fact, if you live in one of the kinds of isolated places that populate Appalachia, there's still a shortage of doctors. "People in rural areas sometimes must travel for hours for care, even in emergencies," (Jaret). And, although, "20% of the of the population lives in rural communities, only 11% of physicians practice in such areas," (Jaret).

"One reason that much of rural America doesn't have enough doctors is that few U.S. medical trainees currently come from rural communities — a problem the medical field also has with doctors of color, and Black doctors in particular, ("In Rural Areas With Health Care Shortages, These Doctors Are Answering the Call").

The more things change, the more things remain the same. Doctors were hard to come by in the Appalachians in 1910 and there is still a shortage of medical personnel in these mountains today.

"In 2017, students with a rural background represented less than 5 percent of all incoming medical students though 17 percent of Americans are considered to be rural," ("In Rural Areas With Health Care Shortages, These Doctors Are Answering the Call").

These mountain folk had to learn how to make do with what they had and if you had a neighbor and could do it, you would help them too.

Midwifery was so important in the hills and hollers of that time, as well as everywhere else. But, for mountain women, there were usually no formally trained doctors available. So, they depended on the granny women to help them have a safe delivery.

Having a baby back then gave an expectant mother a real reason to worry about dying. Mortality rates were very high at the turn of the 20th century. "An American woman in the 18th and 19th centuries had on average seven live births during their lifetimes. The following was written by a woman who had just had her third child in the year 1885. "Between oceans of pain, there stretched continents of fear; fear of death and a dread of suffering beyond bearing."

To get an idea of how deadly childbirth could be, "for every 1,000 live births in 1900, six to nine women died of pregnancy-related complications and approximately 100 infants died before the age of one year," (Childbirth and Babies in the 1900s).

One out of ten children died in childbirth or before the age of one in 1900! I can't imagine the emotional pain these women endured.

I remember being in the old family graveyard, high up on a mountain. And, if you'll notice many graveyards in the mountains are as high up as they could get them. The belief was that the additional elevation literally put them closer to God. I like that thought.

That day, though, I noticed ten little stones sticking up out of the earth. I asked what those were, and my mom told me those stones marked the resting place of ten little souls who were born to my great-granny Nannie; none of them lived to see much life in this world. Most of them were lost in childbirth or before they had a chance to fight their way into this world.

The retelling of one of the losses of these sweet little souls is told below in my mother's own written words.

"Grannie was 13 years old when she married Pap. . .Grannie had 15 babies, but only five lived beyond the age of four.

"Grannie was out alone picking blackberries one day, when she fell and broke her tailbone. This put her right into labor. She was in the ninth month of her pregnancy.

"She crawled and finally got home, too late for the baby. She almost died from loss of blood. Grannie was my second mom," (Roberts, 2003).

These women were so strong, and that strength was given as a special gift to those who have come after them. Once, I had to drive myself to the hospital during a miscarriage of my own, mirroring in a small way my poor great-granny's plight. But I can't imagine what Nannie went through, dragging herself across a mountain to get home. I wonder what kind of care she actually received when she got there. Mom never told me that. I have so many questions now that I wish I could ask her and granny.

If a woman and the child survived the birth during my great-granny's time, then there was a significant chance that she could suffer from lifelong morbidities such as, "vesicovaginal and rectovaginal fistulas from unrepaired lacerations. This could result in lifelong incontinence and vaginal, cervical, and perineal prolapses of these fistulas caused painful sexual intercourse and difficulties with future pregnancies," (Hektoen International).

Being a woman was hard business in those days. Being a woman giving birth was the hardest of all. Mountain grannies brought a little solace, knowledge of herbs,

barks, trees, moss, plants of all ilk, kindness and love to a household on a "granny woman" visit. A midwife/granny woman was worth her weight in gold in those mountains. Before the visit to birth the baby, the woman would have the place all clean, and she'd often have a meal on the stove, as a reward for the granny woman's ministrations that day.

I remember Granny telling me about a woman who had recently had a baby and wasn't able to clear milk out of her breast. The breast got so hard that it split. Granny made up a poultice for her to keep it from getting infected.

Granny (Lennie) helped some people in those mountains, but she couldn't save her son, Buster. This little boy was born with a hole in his heart. Today, it would probably be an easy fix to close the hole, as medicine has advanced so much. I never met Buster, because at the tender age of three, he died shortly before I was born.

Mom said that granny, with very little money, would take the train with Buster all the way to The John Hopkins Hospital in Baltimore, Maryland, hoping that they could do something for him. But, at the time, they couldn't. Buster went into surgery, but his heart began failing. They were able to get him back, but they couldn't do repeat surgery.

Years later, Granny said something that even now, when thinking about it, brings me to tears. "Pat, I just remember Buster being on that old, cold floor because we couldn't get the house warm enough." A lot of those old houses during that time, literally had cracks between the boards. People would often use newspapers as insulation. A West Virginia winter can be a hard thing, with low temperatures and snow measured in feet up in the higher elevations. Like most moms would, Granny carried an enormous amount of guilt because she couldn't save him. If she could have given her own life so he could have lived his, she would have done it in a moment. Mom said that when Buster passed, Granny was never the same.

I didn't know the old granny but loved the one I knew. She had an incredible sense of humor and could keep you laughing for an hour.

I remember granny going on the hunt for asparagus, which grows along the roads in West Virginia, or for blackberries, or "creasy greens," or for any other number of goodies grown by mother nature. But, the best vegetable hunt by folks in the mountains was for ramps.

There should be an ode to the ramp. This tasty and smelly wild leek, paired with bacon, brown beans, and cornbread, is amongst the best dishes I have ever eaten.

And, yes, I have dined at fancy French restaurants. While their dishes have their appeal, they can't compare with the flavor of ramps, fried in bacon fat.

A feature that every granny woman had back in the day, is that they could go into the mountains and bring back an amazing variety of good food to eat and/or natural medicines to use.

These women didn't rely strictly on nature in the wild to survive, they usually had a big garden from which most of their food was sourced. Everything from tomatoes, potatoes, beans, carrots, lettuce, corn, cucumbers, and more, were planted and harvested. The harvest's bounty wasn't a one-time thing, they preserved as much of it as they could.

Granny would say, "Food is medicine," and they had some of the best food I've ever tasted. Until a decade before she passed at the age of 82, if someone had a stomach ache or something else wrong with them, she'd try to patch them up with a tea, tincture, or poultice. Or, she'd tell you how to make it yourself; to heal what ailed you.

Of everyone, granny, had the most effect on me when it came to my worldview, concerning the paranormal and psychic realms. We were very different, but I learned so much from her.

My sister Pam and I talk about how as children, we used to sit at the kitchen table with mom (Alice Roberts) and granny, listening with rapt attention to what these grand old ladies were talking about. They talked about everything, from politics, religion, modern culture, books, all the way to the right way to fix deer venison. We got more relevant information from them than most people get from "Alexa" today.

And, listening to them paid off. When I went away to college I was able to take a CLEP test (College Level Examination Program Course) and tested out of both Fine Arts and the first part of English. I learned more sitting at that kitchen table with Pam, mom, granny, and little sister, Tracey, than I did from my baccalaureate degree.

To this day I am glad that I have these wonderful women in my memories. These were women who didn't have to tell people they were strong, they just were. It was a matter of fact. My great-granny, granny, and mom exemplified the best of the mountain woman. They were smart, capable, cool under pressure, and would do anything they could for their family, and when it was possible, they would help their neighbors. Living in the mountains could be a hard life, but, these women made the best of it and flourished.

Today, I still feel the presence of these ancestors. That presence has influenced me to have a garden, too. It's not nearly as large as granny's and mom's was, but, when I'm working in it, it brings back good memories. I grow a number of herbs, which I love to use in tinctures, potions, and teas. Like mom and grandma, I pay attention to the phases of the moon as to when certain vegetables and herbs are planted.

Amongst my favorite herbs are: basil, rosemary, cilantro, peppermint, thyme, and sage. Right now, in the garden, I have planted: bunching onions, lettuce, cherry tomatoes, tomatoes, carrots, zucchini, cucumbers, and chives. Sunflowers and lavender also grace the landscape of my garden.

The women that came before us in the mountains were probably stronger than we will ever be. But I think they had a strength born out of challenges that many of us no longer have to face, such as geographic isolation, crushing poverty, and having no real voice in the world.

I will forever hold the memories of these wonderful women near to my heart, these granny women of the Appalachian Mountains.

Generations of Grannies

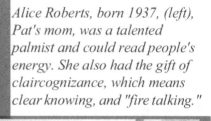

Alice Roberts, born 1937, (left), Pat's mom, was a talented palmist and could read people's energy. She also had the gift of claircognizance, which means clear knowing, and "fire talking."

Lennie Roberts (right), born 1919, Pat's granny, worked successfully with the spirit board. She would often see those who had crossed over in her dreams.

Nannie Crouse Roberts and Pap, Pat's great-grandpap. Nannie had the gift of manifestation and an unshakeable spiritual faith.

Sarah "Sally Fletcher," Pat's great-great grandmother (several generations removed) was born in 1829 and died in 1928, who was the granddaughter of a Choctaw Chief. With her is Morgan Gates.

A scene from the author's Garden.

Chapter 4

The Gift of Second Sight Runs Deep in Mountain Bloodlines

The following are some short vignettes from our lives in the mountains. These stories focus on the supernatural events that happened to us, as I was growing up.

My mother was an amazing woman who had psychic gifts of her own. I am going to share with you just a few of the life events that she wrote about, before she passed. You can see from her stories how gifted and humble she was, which was very common traits amongst many of the descendants of granny women in her generation.

By sharing these treasured stories it shows the connection these mountain people had with the spiritual realm. If ever there were a people who believed in the otherside, it is these folks, (Roberts, 2003). Also covered in this chapter are just a few of the experiences that my grandmother, sisters and I had growing up with the second sight in the Appalachian Mountains.

"Pap, his brother and another young man were out drinking, and tomcattin' around a ways out from Chestnut Ridge. They were riding their horses." When they noticed a man approaching. "One of them said, 'There's a man and he don't have no head.' At about that time, the horses started bucking and almost bucked Pap off. Everybody took to running. When they got home Pap was shaking. From then on, he went the way the crow flies to avoid that road."

Told to my mom, Alice Roberts by Pap, her grandpappy

Mom wrote this about three months before she passed. She was very ill at this point and would soon pass of emphysema. At the time of this event her mother had been dead for several years.

"Mom came to visit me. I'm on a lot of drugs, so maybe it was just in my mind. BUT - I was not thinking about her at the time, it was unexpected. I was watching TV and I felt her warm fingers. It was her hand on my shoulder. I started to turn but knew I wouldn't see her. I think I closed my eyes. I felt warm and at peace, almost like I was in a womb. She put her hand on my forehead and in my mind I heard, 'I'll take your hand.' I knew what she meant and I wanted to go then and she laughed and removed her hand. Except for seeing and holding my babies and Sam (granddaughter), it was the most wonderful experience of my life."

After my mom's encounter with this family spirit she told me, "I heard her say 'soon,' and I said, 'How soon, mom,' then I heard her laugh." When my mom told me this story, I knew I had very little time left with her. I will always be grateful that her mother (my granny Lennie) came to her before she died. When it came time for my mom to go, she crossed over easily.

Mom wrote that this was the most unusual thing to ever happen to her. "One night, I had a toothache. It did hurt, and I prayed, beseeched, and promised how good I would be if only God would stop the pain...to no avail. I was crying in pain. But suddenly, I thought how selfish I was being, and from my heart I said, 'God, I'm so sorry; forgive me. Help a little child in pain somewhere in the world.' With those words, my tooth quit hurting. Maybe the nerves just died, but I've always thought that, God taught me how to pray and taught me how selfish I was, spoiled and selfish."

And, Mom had the gift of second sight. A lot of folks think that it's all fun and games to have these gifts, but sometimes it's a burden to bear.

"One night I was out on the town, and suddenly, I knew someone there was gonna die -- old, selfish me, I thought it was me. I asked my date to take me home (mom was divorced). That night Henry Lewis was murdered, and it was made to look like an accident."

In the early 1960's, Granny and Grandpaw were driving across Renick's mountain when their car was suddenly filled with an intense white light. As they continued to drive down the highway, they realized that they had lost three hours of time. They never figured out as to what happened that made three hours of time disappear. However, the loss of time is a common complaint in UFO abductions.

Granny and the spirit board seemed to have a love/hate relationship. One time she was complaining about what the board was saying, when the board flew out of her hands and hit the wall, doing a slow slide to the floor.

Other people, including myself, had very disturbing experiences in the back bedroom of our house in that little tar paper house in West Virginia, (O'Keefe, 2022). My family was literally terrified of that part of the house.

One evening, I was sitting on the couch watching television when my fiancé at the time grabbed my hand and hurried me out the door. When I asked what was going on, he replied that he had seen a woman walk down the hallway, which he could see from where we were sitting in the living room. There was no one there that day, except me and him.

Fifty years later, I now do psychic and mediumship work around the country, helping people who have loved ones or may have questions about someone who has crossed over. I also do psychic work for others, including working on missing persons cases. If I accept a missing person's case, I never charge. The family whose loved one is missing is already under tremendous pressure. I do this to help pay off my own Karma, which we all have.

It was having these types of unusual and strange occurrences happening around me and having psychically-talented people like my granny and mom in my life that allowed me to be free to explore my own gifts as a child. I owe these Appalachian women more than I could have ever repaid.

Chapter 5

Garden Musings

The joy of a garden! To plant a seed and see it sprout is a reminder of the power of Mother Earth.

Having a garden was very important in the mountains. There were no Piggly Wigglys or Food Lions nearby. It took an almost 40-minute drive from the house we lived in at that time to get to the "big" grocery store. Plus, store-bought groceries were more expensive, so a garden was necessary to survive for many mountain folks.

There was a man who came around with a box truck full of groceries once a week, Mr. Arbuckle. He was one of the best men I ever met. If you needed something special, Mr. Arbuckle would try to find it to bring to you on his next trip around the mountains. Pretty much everyone owed him, like he was rich. I guess I thought he was rich, too. But he wasn't. I was standing at the back of the truck one day, when Mom asked him why he kept running the truck around the mountains delivering stuff to folks. Mr. Arbuckle was well beyond retirement age then. "Well," he said, "there's people in these mountains that have no way to get to town. What would happen to them if I quit?"

Mom told me later that Mr. Arbuckle was featured in the New York Times! I never saw the story, but I sure could see where that could be true.

The last time I heard about him, he had finally closed the back of that old box truck for the last time. He had a nice, cozy little house near Lewisburg, West Virginia. I sure hope he was happy.

A lot of people may have owed Mr. Arbuckle money, but Mom didn't; she had a whole lot of pride. When mom and dad divorced she drove us three girls to Granny's home in West Virginia to live.

We had always spent a lot of time with Granny during the summers. But, this was different, we were now there to live. It was a good life. In many ways, although we were poor and it was hard at times, having granny, mom, and my sisters made it all ok.

One of the reasons I have difficulty understanding why someone can't get above their "raisin'" is because all three of us girls (my two sisters and I) managed to work really hard to avoid getting trapped into poverty.

Tracey and Pam went on to have successful careers in the Army. Tracey retired as a Major and Pam retired as a non-commissioned officer. I am very proud of both of them. The garden was a big reason why we were all well-fed. It was a part of the foundation upon which we were able to have the confidence to leave home with no money in our pockets and do well in the world.

For my mom, though, the garden was a sanctuary. It took her mind off of a lot of worries. She was a single mother and did have a rough go of life then. The local electrician, who mom would pay to do electrical work when we needed it, would catch an earful when he got home from working at our house. Because mom was single and the wife was jealous. Our community was very small, so this sort of information had a way of getting back to us.

But the garden was magickal for her. She tilled, hoed rows, and planted with a reverence that many have for church. But, with mom, she was motivated at times by fear. She was always afraid that she might not be able to keep us kids, because it was hard to provide for us. But, she managed, and the garden seemed to be her reward for working hard to keep her family together.

In late spring, the planting began. By late summer, the harvest was well underway. It used to amaze me that mom could bring in so much food from the garden. Enough to last us all winter long. She and granny would pickle and can hundreds of quart and pint jars. By the end of summer, Mom had created a stocked pantry that a professional chef would envy.

The garden for me is enjoyable. Unlike mom, I have no additional pressures when it comes to gardening, specifically the need to bring in a garden to keep a family alive. I've started gardening again du ring the last two years and I have enjoyed it immensely.

This year, I am turning this special plot of land into a faerie garden. Less vegetables, but more flowers and herbs. I still have all the basics growing, lettuce, tomatoes, cherry tomatoes, zucchini, onions, and more. I have put a small brick patio in, which took me two days to build, and I am working on a nice walkway through the garden. I will add solar lights and a solar water feature, to make this area faerie-worthy. At night, under the soft glow of the lights, this will be a magickal place. This area gives me a place to go to play the steel tongue drum and reflect on the life I have led. A sanctuary that I can share with visitors or family.

We already have a faerie tree on our property, and now we have added a garden to draw the wee folk. The herbs that I will grow from the garden will be used for healing and magick. The vegetables that I will harvest will be used to feed my family.

The magick that I and others reap from this beautiful plot of land is wonderful, indeed.

Anna in the garden.

Garden bounty (below).

Zucchini in bloom (above).

The garden in late spring splendor (below).

Chapter 6

A Bit About Faerie Magick

A Bit About Faerie Magick

I have always felt drawn to the Fae. Even as a child, I had experiences that were so profound that I felt faerie magick was involved in the manifestation of those events.

I am sure that when our Celtic forebears arrived in these great Appalachian mountains. their elementals also joined them from the old countries. Blending with the nature spirits, which were already a part of the landscape.

There was someone else in my life closer to faerie magick than I was. My best friend from childhood was Martha (Marty) Workman. I remember her and I walking down to the creek near her family's old farmhouse. Marty pointed to the creek and told me, "I've seen faeries there several times, Pat." I believed her wholeheartedly, because I knew her, and I could tell that she believed what she said. Even when we were much, much older, she never changed her story, or quit believing that she had seen the fae. She told me that she saw them at the creek, "flying, dancing, and playing music." I loved hearing about Marty's beautiful experiences with the wee folk.

After Marty left this world and passed over into the otherworld, I've often wondered if she is with the wee folk, or if the fae are a part of her new landscape.

One other person I have known personally had a very close relationship with faerie magick and that was the great author and researcher, Rosemary Ellen Guiley. This gracious lady and friend was kind enough to write the introduction to my first book, and for that I will always be grateful. I just re-read her book, Fairy Magic: All about fairies and how to bring their magic into your life. And it pulled at my heartstrings to know how deeply she felt the magick of the fae.

Parallel to our world is an invisible world, the realm of the fairies. The existence of this realm has been known since ancient times the world over. (Guiley, page 4, 2004)

Rosemary Ellen Guiley

Fairy Magic: All about fairies and how to bring their magick into your life

Faerie Tree Spell (page 1 of 2)

For Anna

Items needed:
Tree
Faerie ornaments
A small container

Having a faerie, also spelled fairy, tree is a beautiful way to spend time with children and grandchildren. Through the faerie tree, you can teach the wee ones how to respect and honor both the fae and the natural elements. You can also teach them about magick through this beautiful experience.

A faerie tree can also be created for an adult, of course! The faerie love to be talked to and remembered.

When you first call the faeries at the faerie tree, bring an offering of honey and cream. The Fae love both of them! Place the offerings into the small container that you will take with you. Keep in mind, they usually sleep during the day, but may hear you.

Set the container down, next to the tree, and say the following:

> *Sleep in the day, while others make hay*
> *Play in the night, while others sleep tight.*
> *Be my new friend, as I will be yours*
> *When the moon is above us and you dance in the moors.*

On further trips to the faerie tree, always bring something the faeries love for them. It helps to strengthen your ties with the faeries. They can be a little shy!

In addition to cream and honey, some of the things that faeries love include anything shiny and sparkly. Faeries love the language of gifts, giving and receiving. They may not trust our words, but they may come around through gift-giving.

The one thing that faeries hate is iron! It may not kill them, but it will make them feel sick. So avoid taking anything made of iron to the faerie tree!

My granddaughter and I have spent many hours at our special place. This is a place that she will remember all of her days, a place and a time where she was able to connect with the faeries.

She and I go down to the tree when she visits, and we always bring little trinkets, or images of faeries. Over the years, we've also added birdhouses in the tree and shiny glass trinkets hanging from the branches.

My granddaughter knows the rule about working with the Fae. "Whatever you give to the faeries, you never take back." I've also told her tales of the faerie nations. Her ancestors believed in the fae, and now she does too.

We've sat under the faerie tree and watched birds, butterflies, and squirrels. We watched a toad, and my granddaughter told me that faeries rode on them, like people do on a horse. We talked about how the faeries also used birds to fly upon, like people ride on airplanes. These hours are truly magickal! I recommend a Faerie Tree for everyone's yard!

Faerie Altar Spell

Items needed:

Cream

Honey

Plate

If you would like a special place inside your home to remember your faeries, you can set up a small corner for them. They love being remembered. Don't forget that it is partially through our thoughts and memories that the Fae remain viable in a very cluttered, technologically-glutted world.

You can do something as small as setting out a lovely plate, preferably one that has a flower design on it. Faeries love nature! On the plate, put one or two little images of faeries along with some shiny things. Remember, faeries do not like coins or human money. The energy from these things is very distasteful to them. They love anything else shiny and shimmery! They also like mirrors, so a tiny one would be a wonderful gift, as well as a shiny button or a hair bow. A sparkly piece of prism glass would be a magnificent gift for the fae!

Set a small container on the plate and fill it with cream and a dash of honey. The Fae will be most happy with such a thoughtful gesture.

When you've completed your faerie altar, say the following spell:

> *The faeries dance in the evening light,*
> *Under the moonlight of a bright winter's night.*
>
> *Faeries play in the glens and the dales,*
> *amongst mushroom rings and cat-o-nine-tails.*
>
> *Gossamer wings brush the top of my hand,*
> *Unbeknownst to me as they fly on my land.*

Come into my house as welcome as can be,
As a guest, my wee faeries, in my home you roam free.

Only goodwill you'll give me, as I will do too.
As we build a strong friendship between me and you.

Chapter 7

*Energy, Intent, and Effort
are Important in Magick*

Magick is such a beautiful word! It denotes the idea of creating a bit of reality that did not exist before the spell was cast. Magick is unique to each practitioner. Although Appalachian magick is often created through bone, dirt, words, herbs, crystals, and energy, I am an energy witch, and therefore focus primarily on drawing energy from Divine Energy in my magickal works.

The Appalachian Mountain region is a place that hides many secrets and mysteries amongst its forests, ridges, licks, valleys, gaps, water sources, and hollers. If you are in tune with this energy, you can literally feel a living vibration wrap itself around you when you are in meditation. It is this connection to the mountain energy and the Universal One that gives an energy witch like myself the magick to manifest.

My maternal line has deep ties to the Appalachian Mountains. Generations of my family have lived, survived, and thrived in a geographically isolated region known for its lack of industry and professional opportunities. The region where I lived offered two major employment paths, mining and logging. Both were known for being particularly dangerous industries for workers. My grandpaw, Bol(iver) Roberts (born 1913, died 2002) would travel by horse to a logging camp near Richwoods, WV, stay the week, and travel by the same method home for the weekend. He did that for years. Eventually, he was able to get a job closer to home. My granny Lennie (born in 1919, died 2002) would get up before anyone else and build a fire in the cook stove. When breakfast was finished, she woke granddad and her kids to come to the table before they started their day.

There's an old family story that tells about my granny Lennie using an old mule and a wooden plow to plant a garden. A successful harvest was important, it was what they depended upon to survive the winter. Back then in the mountains, you might go into the nearest town, miles away, maybe quarterly to pick up supplies.

While she was planting the garden by holding onto the reins of the mule that was pushing the plow, she had the youngest baby strapped to her back. She had already corraled her other children into a makeshift fence around a nearby tree.

I've told a lot of folks that we're not the women these amazing grannies were. Those mountain women were tough and strong, physically, mentally, and spiritually. I am very proud to be a descendant of such strong people as my grandparents and mother.

Granny managed to keep her household together, fed, clothed, and housed, with the help of my grandpa. But she also helped others in the community. One story she told me happened when she was still fairly young. My granny got the word that her cousin's wife, from across the mountain was "fixin'" to have her baby. Granny went to help with the birthing. When she got there, she was so mad, she was about to pop. The man, her cousin, had left that poor woman by herself with little ones running around and no food in the pot or kitchen. My mom was a pretty young kid then, but grandma ran her back across that mountain by herself to get some flour, lard, and meat from their larder, so that she could make that woman and those kids something to eat after she helped her have that baby. The baby and momma did just fine, and from what mom told me about that day, they enjoyed that meal!

Granny could help a woman have a baby and also tell that woman her future. Both my granny and mom were psychically gifted. Mom was a palmist, and my grandmother's tool was the Spirit board. I inherited my ability to draw energy from Divine Source for healing and manifestation from these two amazing women, my loving great-grandmother, and others down the family line. I will share with you just one story about one of these women, my Grandma Lennie.

"Amongst my grandma's gifts was the ability to communicate with spirits through the Spirit Board, what is now commonly called a Ouija Board.

"Grandma came out of her bedroom one day, furious. She told me, "Pat, I'm never going to read that ol' board again." I asked her, "What happened"? "Well, Pat," she said, "I asked it if I was going to get my license, and it said I would fail my driving test but get my license. There's no way that could happen." It was an open family secret that she was a terror on the road as a student driver. She had already tried three or four times and had failed the driver's test each time.

"After she completed the test for the upteenth time," the West Virginia State Trooper said, "Mrs. Roberts, you have once again failed your driving test, but I'm going to go ahead and give you your license.

"Grandma also had the gift of mediumship. There were a number of occasions when she talked about having experienced an encounter with someone who had crossed over. She usually encountered these spirits while in the dream state. Like me, she was a raging insomniac. But, when she slept, she would often astral project into the otherworld." (Bussard, et al).

It is from these ancestors that I get my connection to the Appalachian Mountains. In my youth, I would leave in the morning and wander the mountains around my home. I remember camping out with some friends when I was 15 years old. We were poor, poorer than most in a very austere area, so we didn't have camping equipment. I made do with an old blanket and a pillow on the ground. On this camping trip I woke up to something touching my face. My eyes flew open and locked with a deer's eyes, and we both panicked. The deer ran off and I calmed down after realizing who my early morning visitor was. On another trip, while we were leaving and driving down an old, narrow, dusty road, I saw a black bear cub up in a tree and wondered how far away its mom was.

I wanted to share these quick stories with you to show you how close we were to nature. Nature was where we got our food, through our garden and foraging for berries and nuts; our medicine, in part, through foraging; and, our peace, as we gazed out upon those mountains. Nature is magick.

Magickal works have littered the landscape of my life. I will share a couple of examples. When I was 21 years old, I was working full-time in a factory that made curtains. I had worked there on the night shift since I was 16, while attending high school. I was sewing yet another curtain, going through the mechanical motions, thinking, "Is this all my life will be? Will I die here"? At that point, I focused my energy on improving my future in a meaningful way. I looked down at a small table next to my sewing machine, and I saw a college catalog. I didn't remember seeing the catalog sitting there before that moment. The next morning, I called the college and pitched myself to the financial aid director. He told me, "If you can get here and make the grades, Pat, I will keep you here." That phone call changed my life. I went on to earn Associate's, Bachelor's, and Master's degrees. I spent my professional career in Virginia as a journalist, journalism teacher, and college administrator.

In my personal life, it was a magickal spell that brought my husband to me. I did not ask for a specific person in the spell, but rather asked for the energy that would be a match for mine, the energy that I should have with me in this lifetime. Two weeks after casting my spell, I met my handsome husband, and we have been happily together ever since.

For me, magick is a partnership activity that takes place between Universal Energy and your own energy. And, it usually takes effort to have a successful outcome for a spell. In the first example, I had to make that call to the college. I had to find a way to get there and figure out how to survive once I arrived. I worked very hard to manifest what was for me, prior to that fateful call, an impossible dream of earning a higher education. It was magick that opened the door to college, but I had to find my own way there. In the second example, I had to virtually get out of my living room and into the cyberworld by signing-up for a dating site. Something that I had put off doing until that point. Yes, he was literally the only man I dated after my divorce. I was single for three years before I lit that white candle. I've included this beautiful love spell in the spell chapter of this book.

I've curated for you a few of the most successful spells I have cast throughout the years. Remember as you cast, to reach out energetically. Energy, intent, and effort are an important part of every spell!

If you want to find the secrets of the universe, think in terms of energy, frequency and vibration.

Nikola Tesla

Chapter 8

Appalachian Mountain
Superstitions, Signs, and Omens

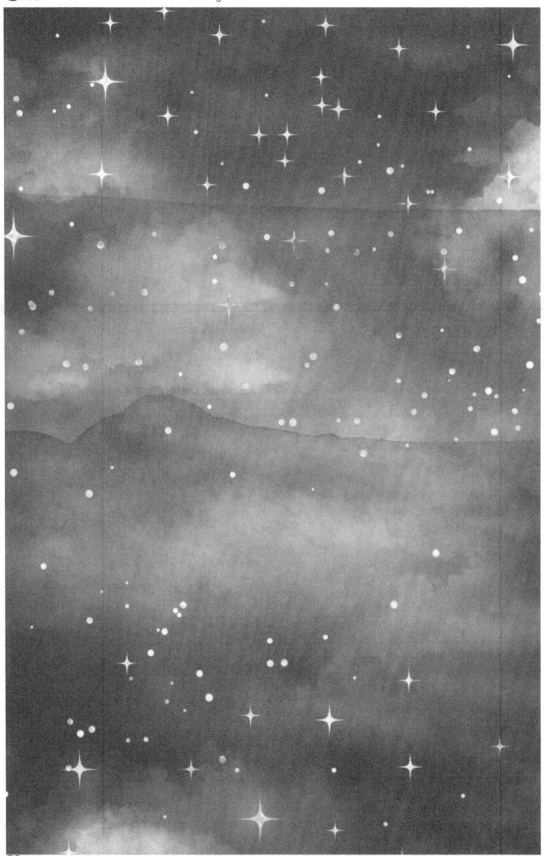

When my ancestors made their way into these mountains from Scotland, England, Ireland, France, Germany, and Norway, they brought with them a number of their superstitions, which are with us today. Superstitions dealing with death, life, nature, water, and more were part and parcel of the everyday life of my granny witch forebears.

What is the difference between superstitions, signs, and omens? A superstition is where you believe that if you do something, it will cause something else to happen. An example is that walking under a ladder will cause you to have bad luck. A sign is when we see something that is a message from the otherworld. An example is finding a white feather, which denotes that the spiritual realm is sending messages of encouragement. An omen is something that foretells the future, either good or bad. An example is that seeing an owl at dusk foretells the death of someone. Of course, these terms are used interchangeably, and that's quite all right. Magick, in all its forms, is not a hard and fast practice. There can be different meanings to different people, the point is that for that person, their own personal meaning makes sense. An example of this is the black cat. In some cultures, it is considered a harbinger of good luck. In other cultures, the black cat is to be avoided at all costs!

Although the topic of Appalachian Mountain superstitions, signs, and omens could be a book in itself, I wanted to share some of them with you since they populated the landscape of my childhood. In this chapter, I am sharing with you some of the superstitions our grannies taught us. Superstitions we may or may not believe to this day.

Black Cats

If you see a black cat cross the road in front of you from right to left, make an X three times. Ensure you have completed the third X by the time the cat has crossed completely. Although I do this because I grew up with my elders "crossing out the bad luck." I truly love cats and have two of them right now. Both of these independent beauties are black in color and their names are Lilith and Luna. A mother and daughter duo.

Some people from Scotland, England, Wales, Ireland, and Germany believe that a cat crossing from left to right is bringing you good luck!

Some folks believe that a black cat walking towards you is bringing good luck with it, while a cat walking away from you is taking good luck with them.

Cats and witches go together like peanut butter and jelly. Cats are synonymous with witches because, during the black plague, it was noticed that women who kept cats, also kept the plague away. Cats, of course, were murderous towards rats, the carriers of fleas that carried the great death. Because she and her loved ones remained uninfected, it looked like the workings of witchcraft!

Spilt Salt

If you spill salt, pitch a bit of it over your left shoulder. Granny always told me it's because negative energy gathers to the left and positive energy to the right. Salt, because it is a preservative, can hurt negative things. Since negative energy rejoices in the fact that such a thing was spilled, it begins to gather to the left of you. So, by throwing a bit of the spilled salt over your left shoulder, you are keeping the bad energy at bay. My granny would say, "You've got an angel to the right of you and ol' scratch to the left of you. Both of them are tryin' to get your attention. Be careful." As I've grown as a magickal being, this information has served me well. Knowing what is good and what is bad energy is imperative when doing energy healing and psychic/ mediumship work. As a lightworker, I have to know immediately if the energy I am working with is from a positive or negative source. Negative energy has a different "feel," even when it is trying to present itself as a positive energy. Negative energy cannot keep up the facade of light and love for a very long time, as it is the antithesis of its own energy.

Doors

Some folks in the mountains thought that entering through one door and exiting through another could bring bad luck. Other folks believed that bad luck could only come only you went out a different door the first time you entered the house.

Telling the Bees

Recently, an old superstition was played out for the late Queen Elizabeth II. The Queen, reportedly an avid bee lover, kept several hives around her garden. When the Queen passed, the bees were informed of her death by her beekeeper, John Chapple. He draped the hives with black ribbon and a bow and then delivered the message. "You knock on each hive and say, 'The mistress is dead, but don't you go. Your master will be a good master to you,' " said Chapple. The telling of the bees is an old tradition dating back to at least the 18th century, if not well before that time. In Celtic lore, bees were believed to have great wisdom and acted as messengers between worlds, bringing back messages from the gods. It is thought that if the bees are not officially told of the demise of their master, they will leave their hive in search of another. Bad fortune could also follow, if someone did not inform the bees of the death of their master. When my grandfather died, he was caretaker to three hives. My grandmother placed a piece of black ribbon on each of the hives and told the bees of their master's death. The bees stayed until they were transferred to another home, as my grandmother could not care for them. The importance of bees in the Appalachians cannot be overstated, certainly to those who had such hard times in these mountains. They brought golden honey to their larder and pollination to their gardens. Both of which made a difficult life, a wee bit better. Telling the bees of their owner's death was an important ritual/superstition to many people in these parts (Maykin).

Brooms

Brooms had special meaning for granny women, in part because they were such a well-used tool for these industrious women. I remember my granny and mom both telling me, "Pat, you can be poor, because that you can't help. But, you don't have to be trash." Through the magick of the broom and other cleaning tools, they always kept a nice and tidy house.

If they wanted to filter out something, say a general feeling of bad energy having come into the house, they would set the broom, with the bristles pointed upwards. This literally filtered out the bad energy and only let the good energy stay. This was also another way to keep company from coming. But, honestly, if someone saw a broom, bristles up standing on the porch and knew the meaning, most folks would just keep walking.

If you didn't want an overnight guest to stay again, you would sweep out the room they had stayed in the minute they were out of the house. This spell works for visitors, as well. The mountain people understood about energy. By sweeping out the energy of the person as soon as they left, it didn't allow any of the person to remain behind.

If a broom fell, it meant that company was coming.

When you move into a new house, always buy or make a new broom. You don't want to bring all that old energy into a new house -- a new house, a new broom, a new start.

Riding brooms are what witches are famous for! There is one theory that witches became associated with riding brooms through indulging in small doses of a fungus that commonly infected rye and created a hallucinogenic state. They were said to have used the end of the broomstick to apply the fungus to the nether regions of their bodies. This was said to have given them serious hallucinations, some of which included flying. Also, in the 1400s a monk named Guillaume Edelin claimed he made a contract with the devil. He told his inquisitors that he had ridden a broom to the location of their meeting.

Another reason for the association of witches flying on brooms is because it would have been something found in every witch's house. And, because magick was involved, what better way to travel (Symbols & Synchronicity)?

Death

Back in the day, death wasn't the scary thing that it is today. People in these mountains didn't have a way to see horror movies of zombies clawing their way out of the earth. Instead, they had a familiar relationship with death. Folks sat with the dying, and the women cleansed the body, and dressed them in their Sunday best for their funeral. The men folk would dig the grave and, after the obligatory three days above ground, to make sure the dead were really dead, make arrangements for the transportation of the body to the gravesite. Their burial ground was many times a little family graveyard located on the property where they died. Other folks were buried in little church graveyards dotted all across the mountains.

If someone wondered if a recently deceased loved one was a witch, they would watch the burial take place. If a frog hopped into the grave, it was a sure sign the loved one was, indeed a witch.

Give an apple to a dying loved one. If they hold the apple through their death and afterwards, it is a rare and marvelous gift. Give the apple to someone with an addiction to alcohol. If they eat the apple, they will be cured.

If a bird flies into the house someone will die.

If you see an owl during the day, someone will die.

Death and bad luck come in threes. I have noticed a pattern in my own life where these things really do seem to come in threes!

If you hear a knock on the door at night three times, someone will die.

Pregnant women should never look at a corpse, because it can mark a child.

Never "grave dance" or walk on graves. The dead will follow you home.

Never leave something where the dead or ghosts dwell, as the ghost can follow you home.

This superstition is one that I adhere to, and there's a reason for that. My granny used to tell me, "Pat, never leave something with the dead, or else they'll know where you live." The warning wasn't about having a ghostly visitor, but more of a new, permanent roommate, so to speak. So, years later, as a psychic and medium and as someone who has investigated a number of haunted places, I made sure to never leave as much as a battery at any known haunted location (or anywhere else, for that matter).

Once, I was at a truly lovely cemetery taking photographs, when I realized I had lost my glasses. In a panic, and with granny's warning ringing in my ears, I looked everywhere for them! I took one last look around a particularly beautiful tomb and found them, geographically centered in the middle of a crosswalk that I had already walked around several times! I truly appreciate the energy that helped me that day.

If you have a dream about a birth, it really denotes a death.

If you dream about a death, it means a marriage. When I was young, I dreamt that my aunt had died and we were all filing past her coffin. It was a very lucid dream. The next morning I told my granny and she said, "Welp, that means she'll marry him then." And, she did.

If someone has lived a good life, flowers will carpet your final resting place. If you have lived a bad life, weeds will take over your grave. You can bet there were a lot of folks out there planting flower seeds over the graves of their loved ones! Appearances mattered for families, even if it had to do with someone in the afterlife.

Remove a corpse from the house feet first so that the recently dead cannot find their way back. Others think that by doing this, they cannot "look" towards those still in the house to lure them into the land of the dead.

When someone dies, they made sure to stop the clock in the house. This is said to prevent a new death (since death and bad luck tend to come in threes). Some people would wait 24 hours before starting the clock again, but Granny waited three days.

And, amongst the most important things to do after someone died, you made sure you or other family members sat with the dead for three days and three nights before burial. Back in the day, folks didn't have the money to get their people embalmed so they would bury them pretty quickly. The reason you sat with them for three days and nights was to make sure they were really dead! During the Victorian era, being buried alive was so common, that they would place a bell above the grave and a string to the bell inside the coffin. So, if the graveyard man heard a bell ringing, he'd know he had some digging to do! This is where we get the saying, "Saved by the bell."

Doctors during the Victorian era had a plethora of things they would do to make sure someone was really dead including the needle flag test. In this, a needle with a small flag attached was thrust into the chest. If the heart was beating, the flag should wave. Many of these methods of ensuring that the once living human was a corpse would be shocking to modern sensibilities. (Alexa)

On the page after next is a poem I wrote years ago titled, "The Watchers." The poem was written while remembering the burial of my great uncle Fred. His was a true Appalachian burial. His casket on sawhorses in the living room, while family members took turns staying up with him for three days and three nights. Many men would tip a drink to him, as they wished him on his way. The women folk worked hard at praying for Fred to be welcomed through the gates of heaven. Hand-played music rarely stopped during those three days.

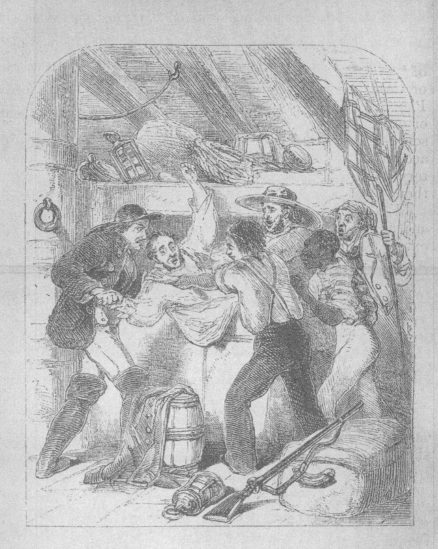

The Premature Burial.

THERE are certain themes, of which the interest is all-
absorbing, but which are too entirely horrible for the
purposes of legitimate fiction. These the mere romant-
icist must eschew, if he do not wish to offend, or to
disgust. They are with propriety handled, only when
the severity and majesty of truth sanctify and sustain
them. We thrill, for example, with the most intense

The Watchers

Watch over me,
The Dead,
as our ancestors did before,
strewing flowers before decay,
decorating our final pallet.
Three Days
of Darkness
Dreadful

Watch for movement
of hand or foot,
of face or limb,
of blinking eye or rasp of breath,
of beating heart or mirror's fog.
Three Days
of Darkness
Dreadful

Watch my body,
blood washed clean,
now, colored by Death's palette,
mottle grays and purples,
As shadows play across gaunt features,
Three Days
of Darkness
Dreadful

Watch as others come,
gathering of family and friends,
Of those who cared and those pretenders,
A viewing, a wake, a goodbye,
fading light on somber faces,

Three Days
of Darkness
Dreadful

Watch over me,
The Dead,
Until the peacocked hearse is gone,
Until the last spade of earth is turned,
Until you release me to the soil,
Three Days
of Darkness
Dreadful.

Boneyard Voice:

Poems and Photographs from the Edge of Darkness

Pat O'Keefe

Chapter 9

Spells & More
From the Spellbook
of an Appalachian Mountain Witch

Magick in the Appalachian
Mountains runs deep.

The Goddess Hecate

Using a Greek goddess to illustrate each page of spells in this book, for an Appalachian witch, may seem odd at first. But, The Goddess Hecate was one of the female energies of the Greek Pantheon that I became very interested in as a child, as she was said to be extremely wise and was the goddess of magick. As a child with a vivid imagination, she made quite an impression. I loved that her energy was so powerful, yet so feminine at the same time.

Gazing from the top of each of the pages of spells in this book is an artistic depiction of the Greek Goddess Hecate. Examples of those images are to the left. Goddess Hecate is known as the goddess of magick, witches, the night, the moon, ghosts, and necromancy.

As she is the goddess of magick, what better figure to "overlook" each page of magick in this book!

Goddess Hecate is said to be a triple goddess, representing the maid, mother, and crone. All of the phases of a woman's life are personified in her.

She wanders the night with her hounds, holding a pair of torches. As the goddess of the crossroads, the skeleton key represents her dominion over the gates to all realms.

The Author's Book of Shadows

NOTE: In my spellwork I like to keep things simple so that I
can work with focused intent and energy.
Other folks may like more complex
spellwork, and that's ok too. There
are many ways to the center.
Find what works for you!

Spells & More

Spells & More
Table of Contents

Table of Contents for Spells & More continued on the next page.

Spells & More
Table of Contents
(Continued)

Spells & More
Table of Contents
(Continued)

Banishing
+ Hexing
Spells

Banish a Person Spell

Items needed:
Lavender oil
Paper
Pen

Write a person's name on a piece of paper. Fold the paper up, making sure you fold it away from you. Drop a bit of lavender oil on all four ends of the paper. Shake off any excess.

Take the piece of paper and bury it away from the house. As the paper dissolves back into the earth, the person that you have banished will dissolve from your life.

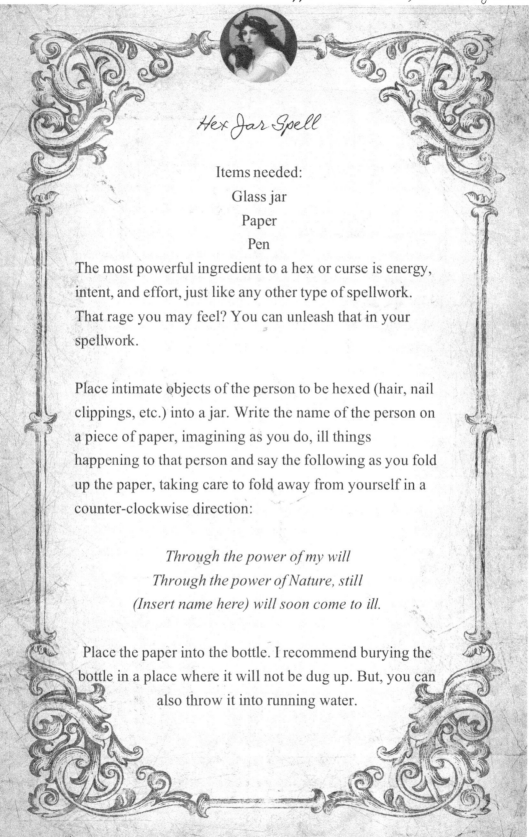

Hex Jar Spell

Items needed:

Glass jar

Paper

Pen

The most powerful ingredient to a hex or curse is energy, intent, and effort, just like any other type of spellwork. That rage you may feel? You can unleash that in your spellwork.

Place intimate objects of the person to be hexed (hair, nail clippings, etc.) into a jar. Write the name of the person on a piece of paper, imagining as you do, ill things happening to that person and say the following as you fold up the paper, taking care to fold away from yourself in a counter-clockwise direction:

Through the power of my will
Through the power of Nature, still
(Insert name here) will soon come to ill.

Place the paper into the bottle. I recommend burying the bottle in a place where it will not be dug up. But, you can also throw it into running water.

General Banishment Spell

Item needed:

1 Apple

Cut the apple in half, so that the star is showing. Take mint and place it between the two pieces. Skewer the pieces together. Then, wrap a black cloth around the skewered apple. As you wrap the black cloth around the apple, say the following:

_____ *is banished from my life*
That which gave me pain and strife
Like this apple, returns to earth.
It has no hold and no worth.

So mote it be.

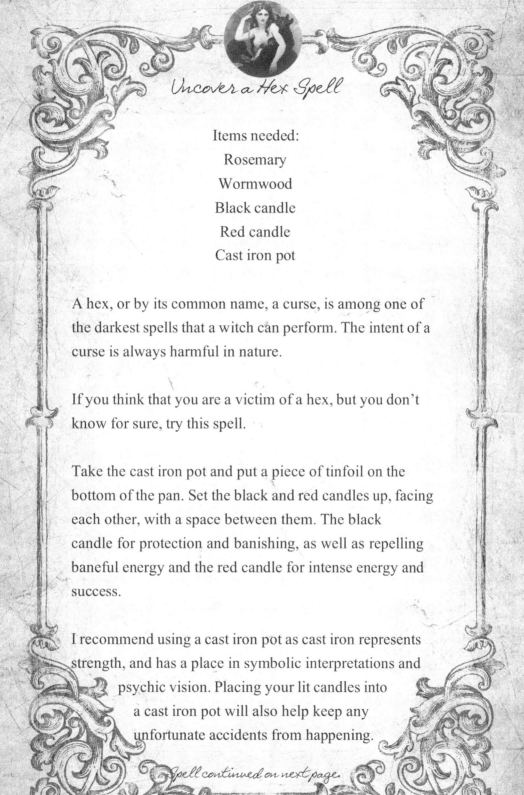

Uncover a Hex Spell

Items needed:
Rosemary
Wormwood
Black candle
Red candle
Cast iron pot

A hex, or by its common name, a curse, is among one of the darkest spells that a witch can perform. The intent of a curse is always harmful in nature.

If you think that you are a victim of a hex, but you don't know for sure, try this spell.

Take the cast iron pot and put a piece of tinfoil on the bottom of the pan. Set the black and red candles up, facing each other, with a space between them. The black candle for protection and banishing, as well as repelling baneful energy and the red candle for intense energy and success.

I recommend using a cast iron pot as cast iron represents strength, and has a place in symbolic interpretations and psychic vision. Placing your lit candles into a cast iron pot will also help keep any unfortunate accidents from happening.

Spell continued on next page.

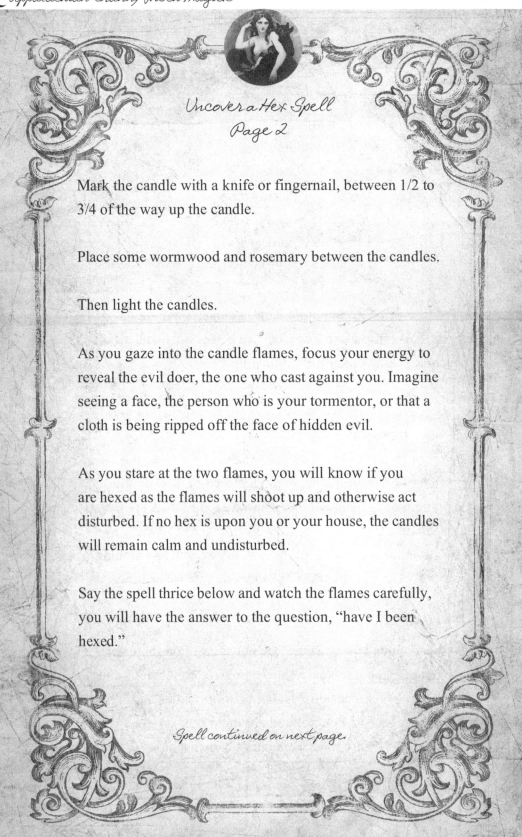

Uncover a Hex Spell
Page 2

Mark the candle with a knife or fingernail, between 1/2 to 3/4 of the way up the candle.

Place some wormwood and rosemary between the candles.

Then light the candles.

As you gaze into the candle flames, focus your energy to reveal the evil doer, the one who cast against you. Imagine seeing a face, the person who is your tormentor, or that a cloth is being ripped off the face of hidden evil.

As you stare at the two flames, you will know if you are hexed as the flames will shoot up and otherwise act disturbed. If no hex is upon you or your house, the candles will remain calm and undisturbed.

Say the spell thrice below and watch the flames carefully, you will have the answer to the question, "have I been hexed."

Spell continued on next page.

Uncover a Hex Spell
Page 3

Within these flames may be revealed,
dark magick cast against me.
Whether flame will glow
or burn real slow.
Evil cannot deceive me.

Charging
+ Protecting
Magickal Tools

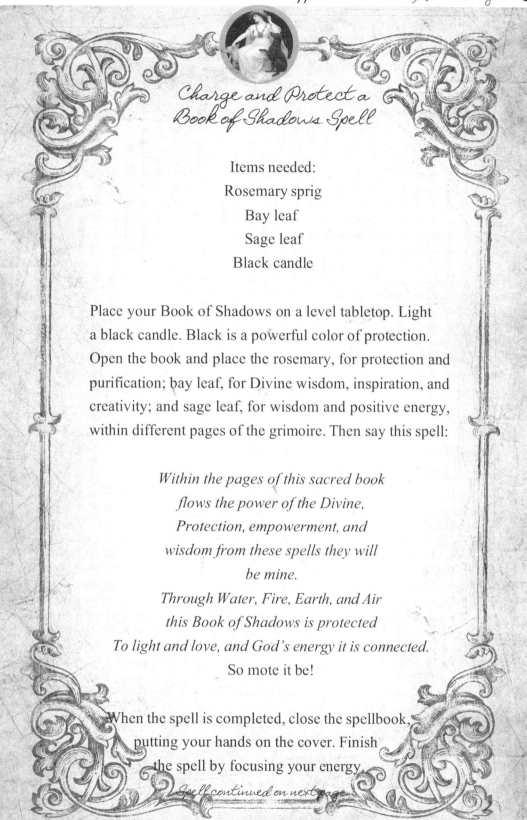

Charge and Protect a Book of Shadows Spell

Items needed:
Rosemary sprig
Bay leaf
Sage leaf
Black candle

Place your Book of Shadows on a level tabletop. Light a black candle. Black is a powerful color of protection. Open the book and place the rosemary, for protection and purification; bay leaf, for Divine wisdom, inspiration, and creativity; and sage leaf, for wisdom and positive energy, within different pages of the grimoire. Then say this spell:

Within the pages of this sacred book
flows the power of the Divine,
Protection, empowerment, and
wisdom from these spells they will
be mine.
Through Water, Fire, Earth, and Air
this Book of Shadows is protected
To light and love, and God's energy it is connected.
So mote it be!

When the spell is completed, close the spellbook, putting your hands on the cover. Finish the spell by focusing your energy.

Spell continued on next page

Charge and Protect a Book of Shadows Spell
Page 2

and imagining light surrounding this book of shadows, one the most important of the tools of a witch of any variety.

Dispose of the remnants of the black candle.

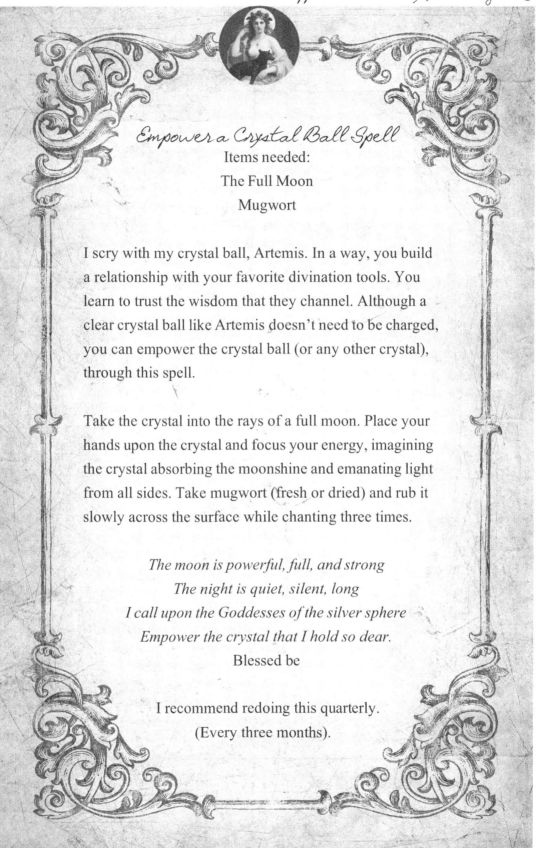

Empower a Crystal Ball Spell

Items needed:

The Full Moon

Mugwort

I scry with my crystal ball, Artemis. In a way, you build a relationship with your favorite divination tools. You learn to trust the wisdom that they channel. Although a clear crystal ball like Artemis doesn't need to be charged, you can empower the crystal ball (or any other crystal), through this spell.

Take the crystal into the rays of a full moon. Place your hands upon the crystal and focus your energy, imagining the crystal absorbing the moonshine and emanating light from all sides. Take mugwort (fresh or dried) and rub it slowly across the surface while chanting three times.

The moon is powerful, full, and strong
The night is quiet, silent, long
I call upon the Goddesses of the silver sphere
Empower the crystal that I hold so dear.
Blessed be

I recommend redoing this quarterly.
(Every three months).

Spells for
Babies
• Children

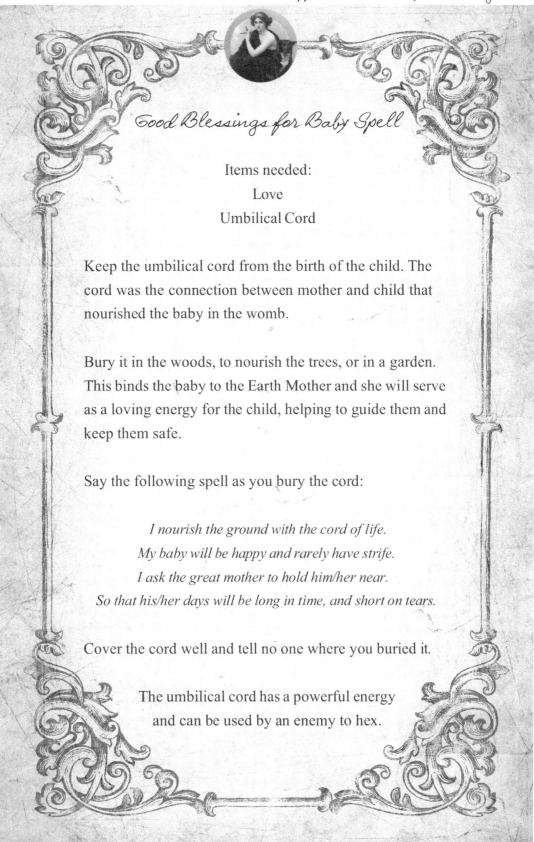

Good Blessings for Baby Spell

Items needed:
Love
Umbilical Cord

Keep the umbilical cord from the birth of the child. The cord was the connection between mother and child that nourished the baby in the womb.

Bury it in the woods, to nourish the trees, or in a garden. This binds the baby to the Earth Mother and she will serve as a loving energy for the child, helping to guide them and keep them safe.

Say the following spell as you bury the cord:

I nourish the ground with the cord of life.
My baby will be happy and rarely have strife.
I ask the great mother to hold him/her near.
So that his/her days will be long in time, and short on tears.

Cover the cord well and tell no one where you buried it.

The umbilical cord has a powerful energy
and can be used by an enemy to hex.

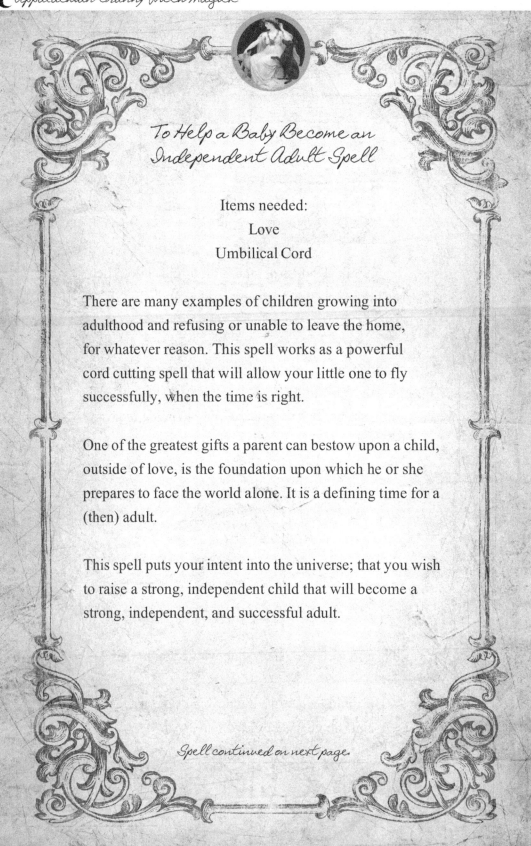

To Help a Baby Become an Independent Adult Spell

Items needed:

Love

Umbilical Cord

There are many examples of children growing into adulthood and refusing or unable to leave the home, for whatever reason. This spell works as a powerful cord cutting spell that will allow your little one to fly successfully, when the time is right.

One of the greatest gifts a parent can bestow upon a child, outside of love, is the foundation upon which he or she prepares to face the world alone. It is a defining time for a (then) adult.

This spell puts your intent into the universe; that you wish to raise a strong, independent child that will become a strong, independent, and successful adult.

Spell continued on next page.

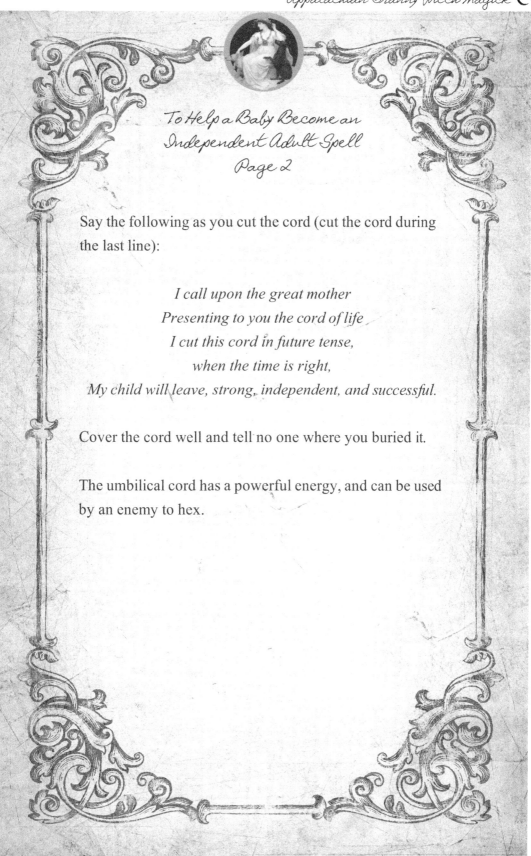

*To Help a Baby Become an
Independent Adult Spell
Page 2*

Say the following as you cut the cord (cut the cord during the last line):

> *I call upon the great mother*
> *Presenting to you the cord of life*
> *I cut this cord in future tense,*
> *when the time is right,*
> *My child will leave, strong, independent, and successful.*

Cover the cord well and tell no one where you buried it.

The umbilical cord has a powerful energy, and can be used by an enemy to hex.

To Keep a Baby Safe from Faeries Spell

Items needed:

Iron nail

In faerie lore, it is said that they can take a healthy human baby and replace it with a sickly faerie child. These children were known as changelings. It was a common story amongst our Irish ancestors.

This spell helps protect that child from becoming a changeling.

Faeries hate iron! Take an iron nail and place it (in a bag for baby's safety) underneath the crib mattress. You could also lay it on the floor underneath the crib, unless you have animals or a crawling/walking baby who could hurt themselves on the nail.

If a baby shares a family bed at times, you can also place one underneath the mattress of the bed.

Spell continued on next page.

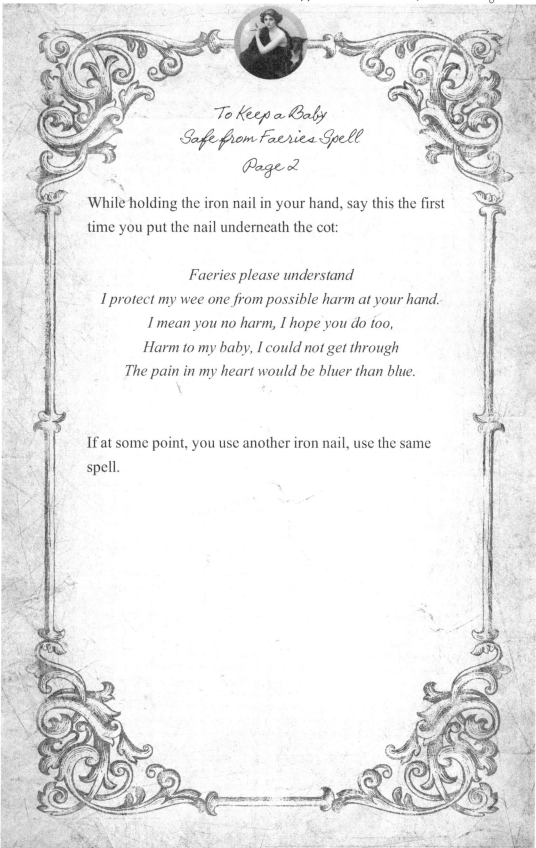

*To Keep a Baby
Safe from Faeries Spell
Page 2*

While holding the iron nail in your hand, say this the first time you put the nail underneath the cot:

*Faeries please understand
I protect my wee one from possible harm at your hand.
I mean you no harm, I hope you do too,
Harm to my baby, I could not get through
The pain in my heart would be bluer than blue.*

If at some point, you use another iron nail, use the same spell.

To Keep Your Child Close to You in Their Heart Spell

Items needed:
Honey

Place a photograph of the child on a plate and pour honey over it. Make sure that the photo is covered, front and back.

Take the plate with the honey-covered photo away from the house, as it could draw ants.

Say the following spell as you are burying the photograph under a tree or bush:

Keep my child close to me in their heart
As they grow older and may move far apart

The honey works as a sticky "binder" that will keep you close in your child's heart, even when they are now an adult and have begun a life of their own.

Find
Something
Spells

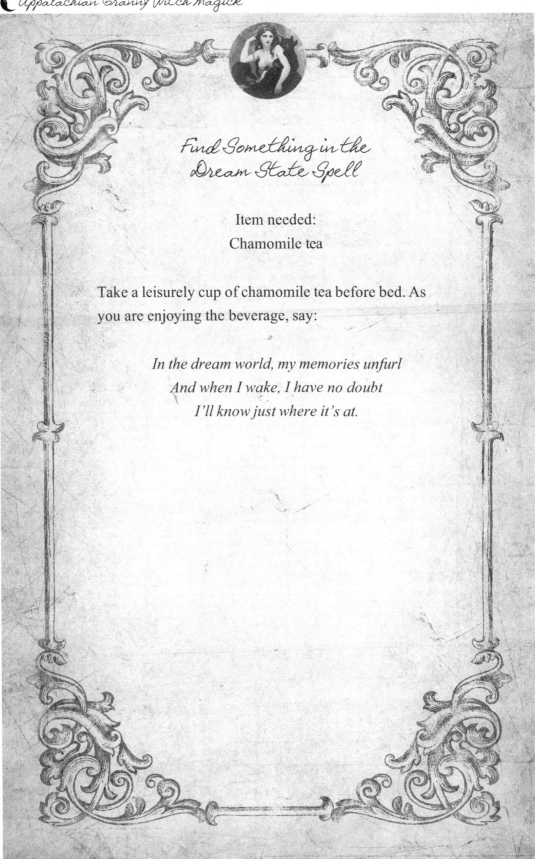

Find Something in the Dream State Spell

Item needed:
Chamomile tea

Take a leisurely cup of chamomile tea before bed. As you are enjoying the beverage, say:

In the dream world, my memories unfurl
And when I wake, I have no doubt
I'll know just where it's at.

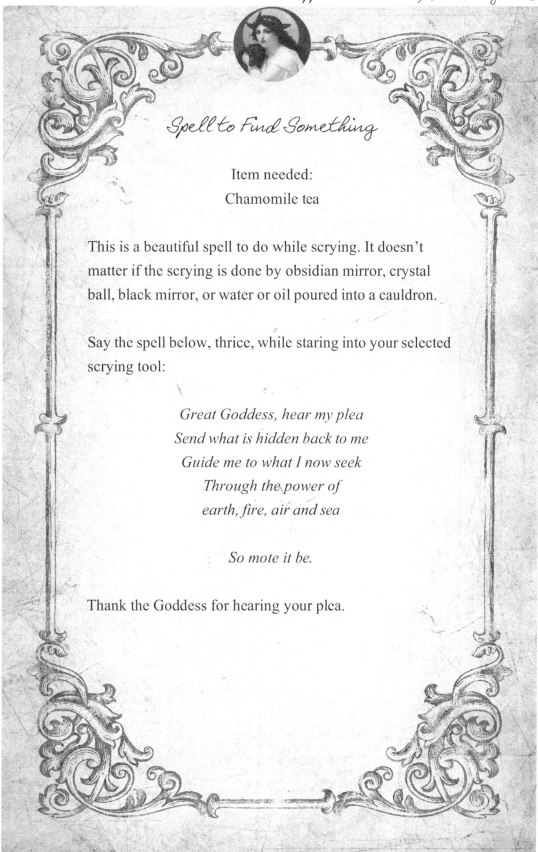

Spell to Find Something

Item needed:
Chamomile tea

This is a beautiful spell to do while scrying. It doesn't matter if the scrying is done by obsidian mirror, crystal ball, black mirror, or water or oil poured into a cauldron.

Say the spell below, thrice, while staring into your selected scrying tool:

Great Goddess, hear my plea
Send what is hidden back to me
Guide me to what I now seek
Through the power of
earth, fire, air and sea

So mote it be.

Thank the Goddess for hearing your plea.

Full Moon
Spells

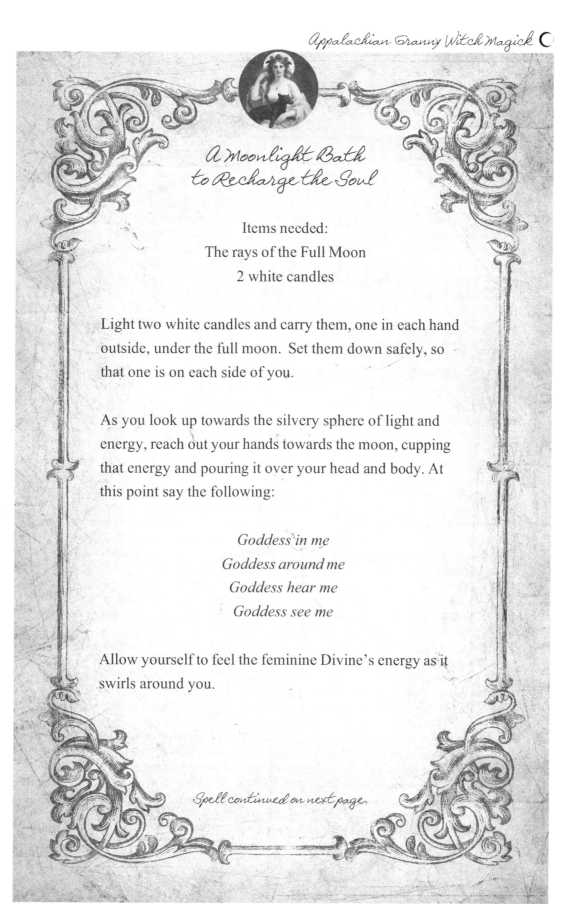

A Moonlight Bath to Recharge the Soul

Items needed:
The rays of the Full Moon
2 white candles

Light two white candles and carry them, one in each hand outside, under the full moon. Set them down safely, so that one is on each side of you.

As you look up towards the silvery sphere of light and energy, reach out your hands towards the moon, cupping that energy and pouring it over your head and body. At this point say the following:

Goddess in me
Goddess around me
Goddess hear me
Goddess see me

Allow yourself to feel the feminine Divine's energy as it swirls around you.

Spell continued on next page.

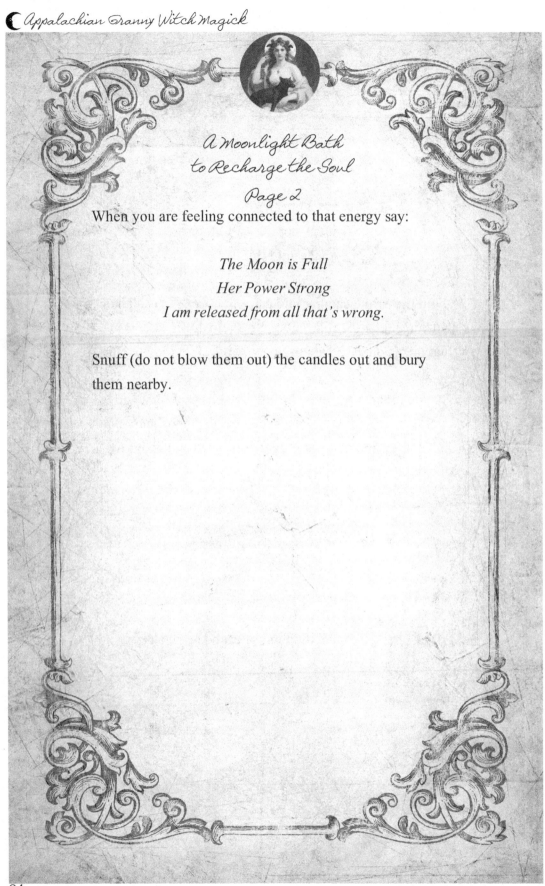

A Moonlight Bath
to Recharge the Soul

Page 2

When you are feeling connected to that energy say:

The Moon is Full
Her Power Strong
I am released from all that's wrong.

Snuff (do not blow them out) the candles out and bury them nearby.

Full Moon Magick

Items needed:
Full Moon

Who doesn't love a full moon? I adore this time of the cycle of the moon, even though it does tend to make my insomnia go out of control.

Here are a few things that I do on a full moon that are easy and have amazing results.

Putting my crystals out under the full moon to absorb the energy of the moon is one way I use this energy. I can literally feel the difference in some of my crystals after they've spent a night outside under the rays of the moon.

I will also put some of my metaphysical tools outside the night when the moon is fullest. The lovely silver streaming from this ancient orb is shared with these tools so that they are able to absorb that energy.

I will sometimes sit under the full moon to feel that energy wash over me, cleansing my energy. There is a more detailed full moon spell in this spellbook, Moonlight Bath Spell.

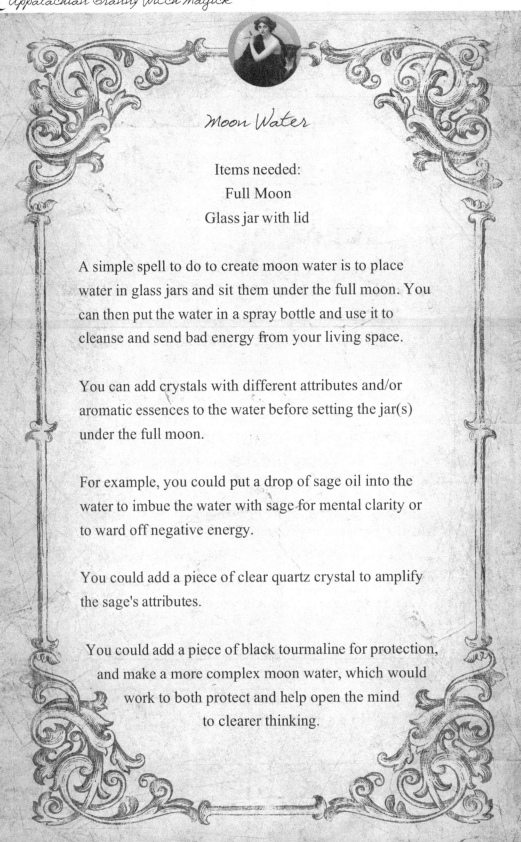

Moon Water

Items needed:

Full Moon

Glass jar with lid

A simple spell to do to create moon water is to place water in glass jars and sit them under the full moon. You can then put the water in a spray bottle and use it to cleanse and send bad energy from your living space.

You can add crystals with different attributes and/or aromatic essences to the water before setting the jar(s) under the full moon.

For example, you could put a drop of sage oil into the water to imbue the water with sage for mental clarity or to ward off negative energy.

You could add a piece of clear quartz crystal to amplify the sage's attributes.

You could add a piece of black tourmaline for protection, and make a more complex moon water, which would work to both protect and help open the mind to clearer thinking.

Ghost
Spells

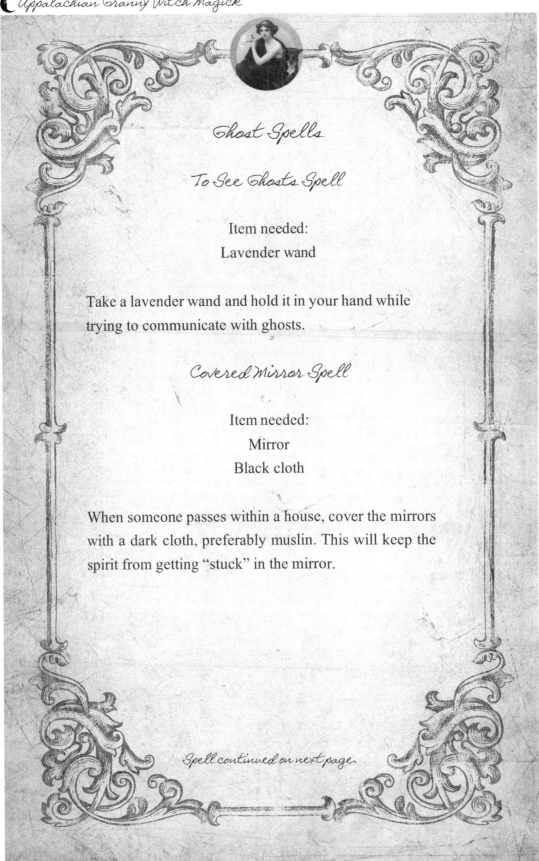

Ghost Spells

To See Ghosts Spell

Item needed:
Lavender wand

Take a lavender wand and hold it in your hand while trying to communicate with ghosts.

Covered Mirror Spell

Item needed:
Mirror
Black cloth

When someone passes within a house, cover the mirrors with a dark cloth, preferably muslin. This will keep the spirit from getting "stuck" in the mirror.

Spell continued on next page.

Ghost Spells
Continued, Page 2

Prevent Ghosts Spell

Item needed:
Raspberry vines

Place vines over the entrance to the deceased's door. This
will keep the deceased from coming back to haunt their
old home.

Expel Ghosts Spell

Item needed:
Salt water

Spray salt water from each corner of the room, towards
an open window, saying names of power. When you have
cleared everything out the window, spray the salt water
across the window seal. End with the phrase, "Blessed
be," and close the window.

Love
Spells

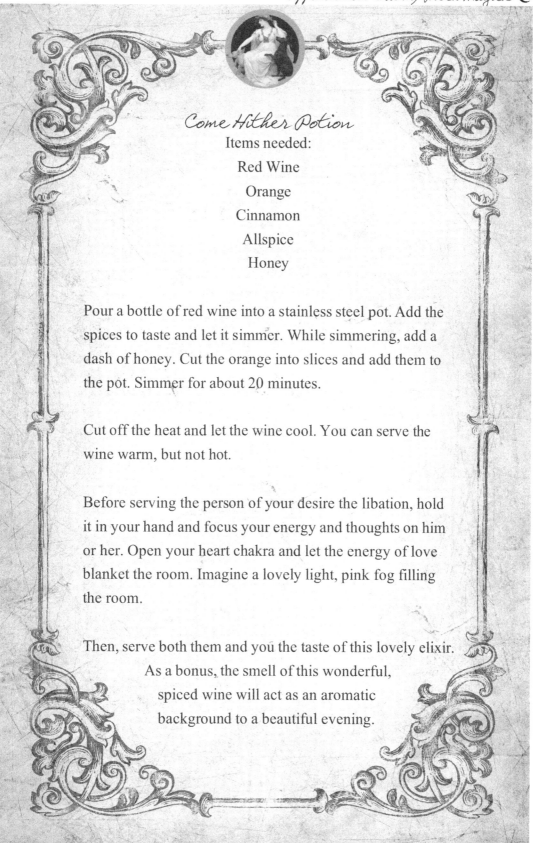

Come Hither Potion

Items needed:

Red Wine

Orange

Cinnamon

Allspice

Honey

Pour a bottle of red wine into a stainless steel pot. Add the spices to taste and let it simmer. While simmering, add a dash of honey. Cut the orange into slices and add them to the pot. Simmer for about 20 minutes.

Cut off the heat and let the wine cool. You can serve the wine warm, but not hot.

Before serving the person of your desire the libation, hold it in your hand and focus your energy and thoughts on him or her. Open your heart chakra and let the energy of love blanket the room. Imagine a lovely light, pink fog filling the room.

Then, serve both them and you the taste of this lovely elixir. As a bonus, the smell of this wonderful, spiced wine will act as an aromatic background to a beautiful evening.

For Love Spell

Items needed:
White candle
Pink quartz

NOTE: Never ask for a specific man or woman, which some witches see as dark magick, as you are bending someone's free will to your bidding. Nor ask for specific attributes or qualities. The Goddess sees the heart and knows who that very special person should be in your life.

Take a white tealight candle, a piece of pink quartz and set them together on your altar or on a table.

Light the candle and focus intently upon the words of the spell, opening your heart up to the Universal Feminine Force. Let her know that you simply want love.

Great Goddess, bring into my life and heart, the man (or woman) who was supposed to be with me in this lifetime. The man/woman who will complete me on a soul-level to bring me happiness and contentment.

So mote it be.

Spell continued on next page.

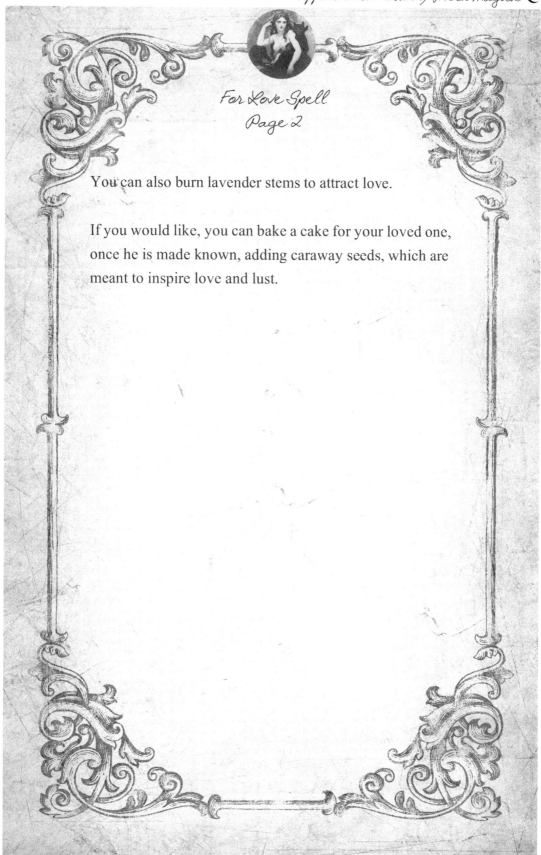

For Love Spell
Page 2

You can also burn lavender stems to attract love.

If you would like, you can bake a cake for your loved one, once he is made known, adding caraway seeds, which are meant to inspire love and lust.

Intensify Love Spell

Items needed:
Pink candle
pink quartz
Rose oil

Put a piece of pink quartz next to the candle and it should remain there during the spell.

Pick up the candle and anoint it with the rose oil (only put it on the wax). As you are anointing the candle say the following spell:

From my heart to his/hers, from his/hers to mine.
Love forever, love in kind.

My heart is warm, open, true
His heart is filled with love for me, too.

Close we are, closer we'll be,
Our love is as powerful as an endless sea.

So mote it be.

When you light the candle, say the spell again.

Light the candle and let the candle
burn completely down.

Spell continued on next page.

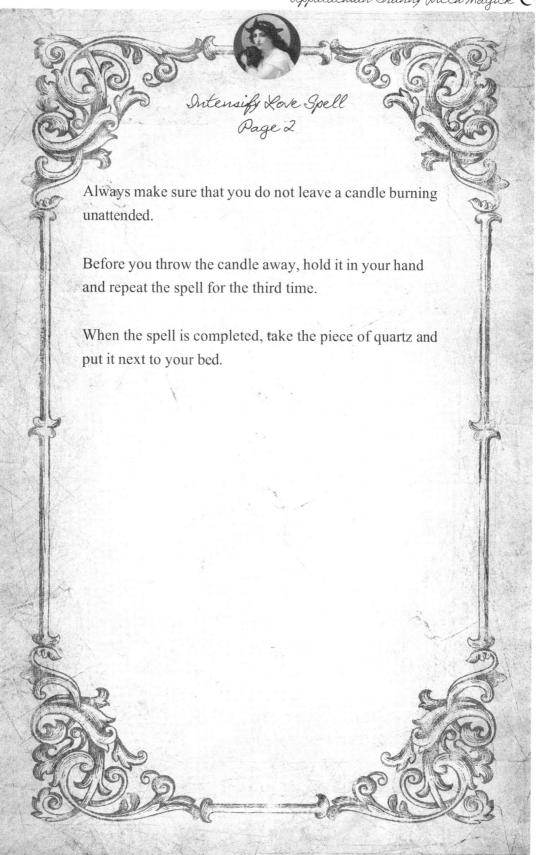

Intensify Love Spell
Page 2

Always make sure that you do not leave a candle burning unattended.

Before you throw the candle away, hold it in your hand and repeat the spell for the third time.

When the spell is completed, take the piece of quartz and put it next to your bed.

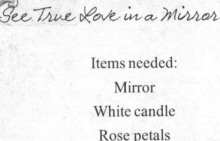

See True Love in a Mirror Spell

Items needed:
Mirror
White candle
Rose petals

Light a white candle and place it next to a mirror on a flat surface near midnight. Take fresh rose petals and scatter them about the surface where the mirror is placed.

Stare into the mirror, focus your energy, reaching out to your future mate and say, thrice at the stroke of midnight:

The mirror is a doorway and will reveal
my true love, who will come to be.
I see his face, his love I feel,
He will find his way to me.

So mote it be.

Be patient, stare deeply into the mirror. After the spell has come to fruition and you see the face of your future love. Blow out the candle. Dispose of the candle, take the rose petals, lay them out to dry. Once they are dried, put them into a small bag and keep them in your purse or bedroom, near your bed.

Spell continued on next page.

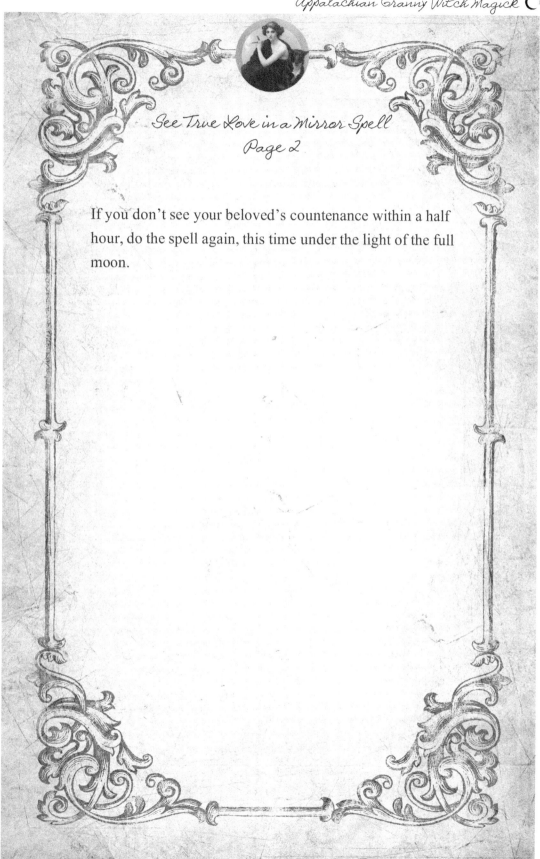

See True Love in a Mirror Spell
Page 2

If you don't see your beloved's countenance within a half hour, do the spell again, this time under the light of the full moon.

Prosperity
Spells

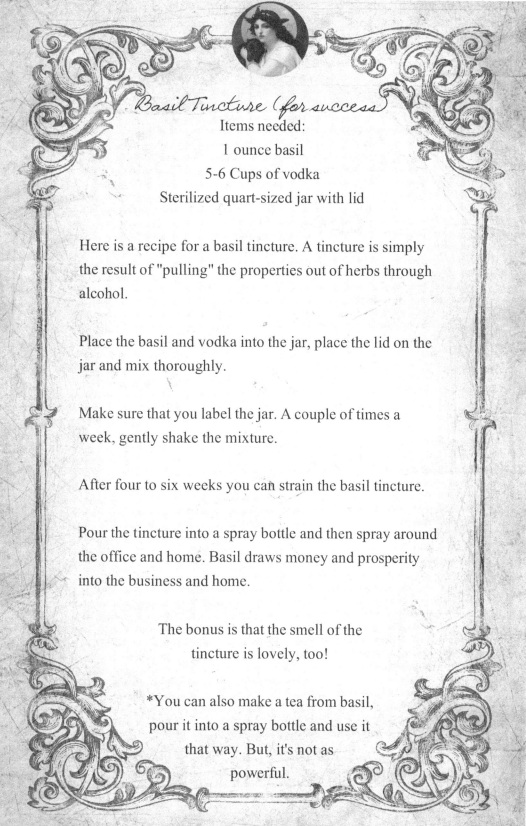

Basil Tincture (for success)

Items needed:

1 ounce basil

5-6 Cups of vodka

Sterilized quart-sized jar with lid

Here is a recipe for a basil tincture. A tincture is simply the result of "pulling" the properties out of herbs through alcohol.

Place the basil and vodka into the jar, place the lid on the jar and mix thoroughly.

Make sure that you label the jar. A couple of times a week, gently shake the mixture.

After four to six weeks you can strain the basil tincture.

Pour the tincture into a spray bottle and then spray around the office and home. Basil draws money and prosperity into the business and home.

The bonus is that the smell of the tincture is lovely, too!

*You can also make a tea from basil, pour it into a spray bottle and use it that way. But, it's not as powerful.

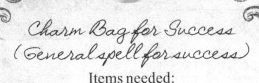

Charm Bag for Success
(General spell for success)

Items needed:

Basil

Rosemary

Thyme

Oregano

It's amazing what we have in our kitchen cupboards that have so much magick in them!

Take these common herbs, place some of each in a small red drawstring bag. Close the bag.

As you are closing the bag, focus on your desired outcome for success. Focus the mind and imagine that your success has already happened. Feel it. Live it. Work for it. You've already put energy into the universe to "clear the way" for future success.

Always remember, we must do our part in our magickal works to make our intent manifest in the way we envisioned.

Basil brings love
Rosemary protects
Thyme gives courage and strength,
Oregano brings joy, wealth, and luck!

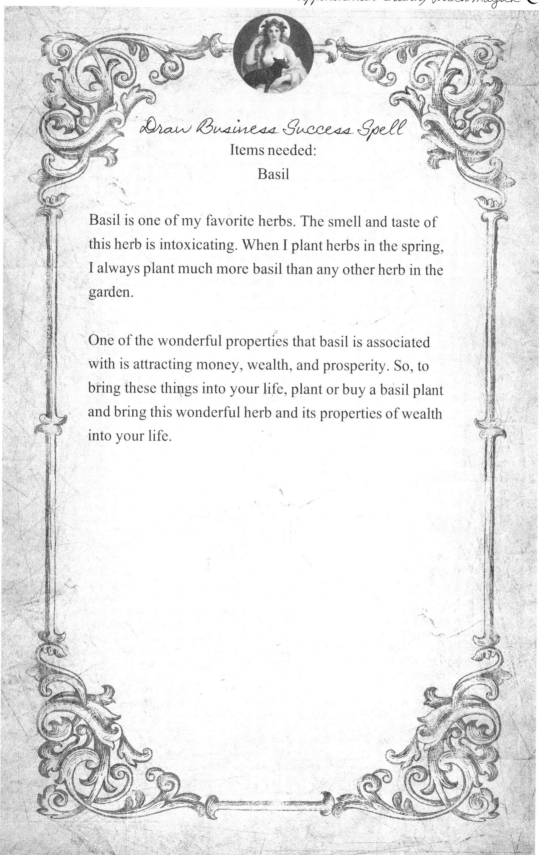

Draw Business Success Spell

Items needed:

Basil

Basil is one of my favorite herbs. The smell and taste of this herb is intoxicating. When I plant herbs in the spring, I always plant much more basil than any other herb in the garden.

One of the wonderful properties that basil is associated with is attracting money, wealth, and prosperity. So, to bring these things into your life, plant or buy a basil plant and bring this wonderful herb and its properties of wealth into your life.

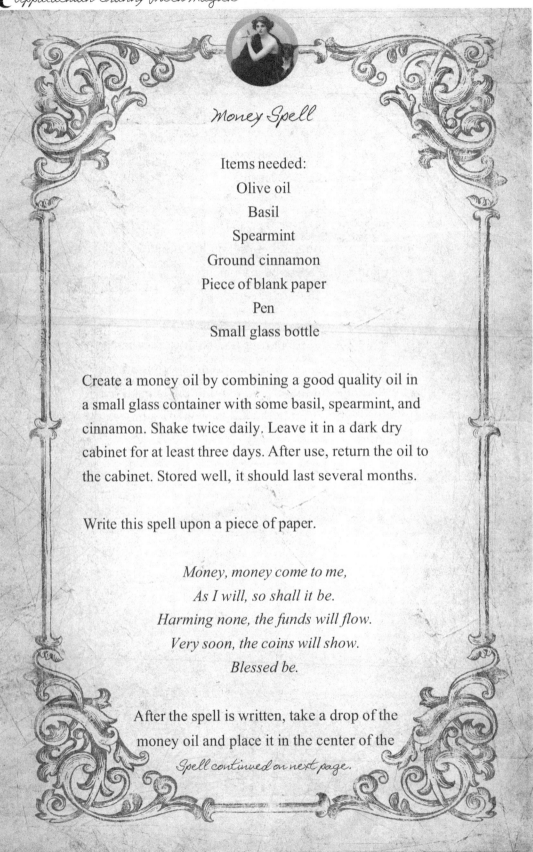

Money Spell

Items needed:
Olive oil
Basil
Spearmint
Ground cinnamon
Piece of blank paper
Pen
Small glass bottle

Create a money oil by combining a good quality oil in a small glass container with some basil, spearmint, and cinnamon. Shake twice daily. Leave it in a dark dry cabinet for at least three days. After use, return the oil to the cabinet. Stored well, it should last several months.

Write this spell upon a piece of paper.

Money, money come to me,
As I will, so shall it be.
Harming none, the funds will flow.
Very soon, the coins will show.
Blessed be.

After the spell is written, take a drop of the money oil and place it in the center of the

Spell continued on next page.

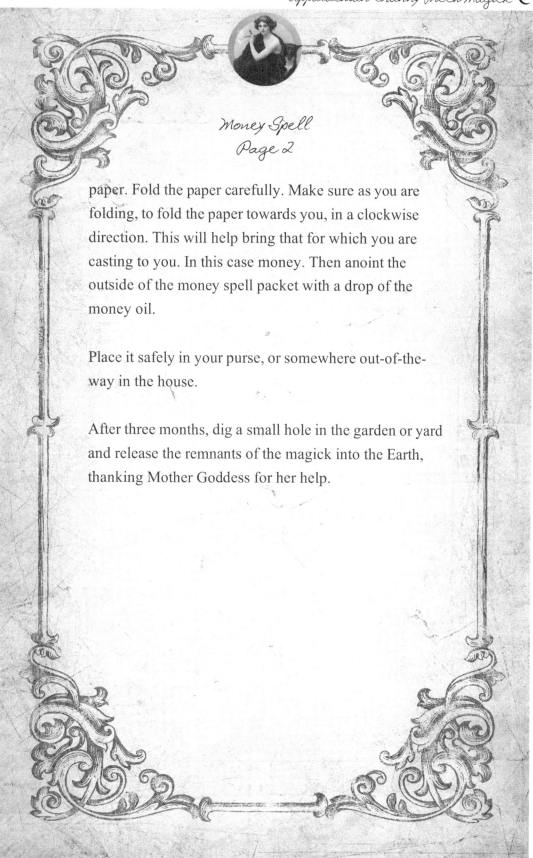

Money Spell
Page 2

paper. Fold the paper carefully. Make sure as you are folding, to fold the paper towards you, in a clockwise direction. This will help bring that for which you are casting to you. In this case money. Then anoint the outside of the money spell packet with a drop of the money oil.

Place it safely in your purse, or somewhere out-of-the-way in the house.

After three months, dig a small hole in the garden or yard and release the remnants of the magick into the Earth, thanking Mother Goddess for her help.

Prosperity Spell

Items needed:
Green candle
Frankincense
Sweet orange
Lemon/Lemongrass

Another version of money oil is to combine a good quality oil with a bit of frankincense, sweet orange, Lemon or Lemongrass. Shake twice daily. Leave it in a dark dry cabinet for at least three days. After use, return the oil to the cabinet. Stored well, it should last several months.

This simple spell is best done with a coven of people holding hands, sitting at a table. But it can be cast by a single practitioner.

Light a green candle that was anointed with money oil (either this version or the one described in the money spell on the previous page).

Say the following spell, 3 x 3, or
until you feel the need to release the energy.

Spell continued on next page.

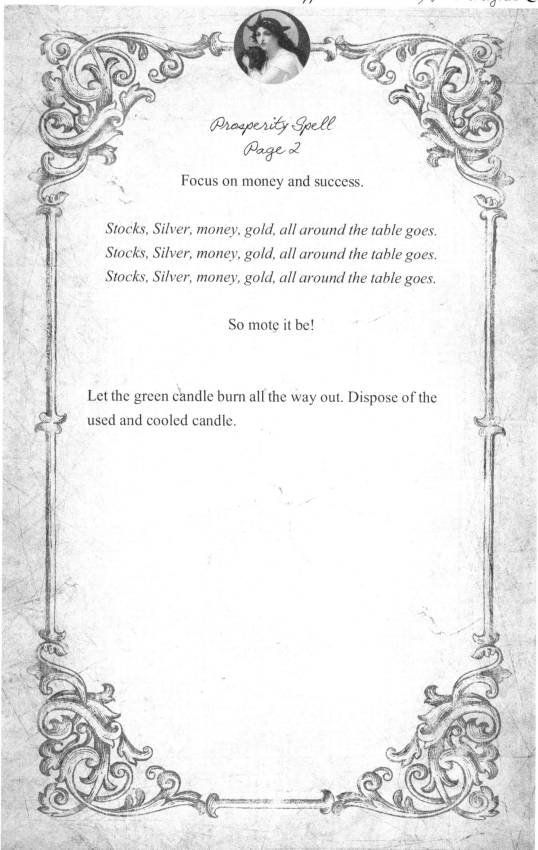

Prosperity Spell
Page 2

Focus on money and success.

Stocks, Silver, money, gold, all around the table goes.
Stocks, Silver, money, gold, all around the table goes.
Stocks, Silver, money, gold, all around the table goes.

So mote it be!

Let the green candle burn all the way out. Dispose of the used and cooled candle.

Protection
+ Truth
Spells

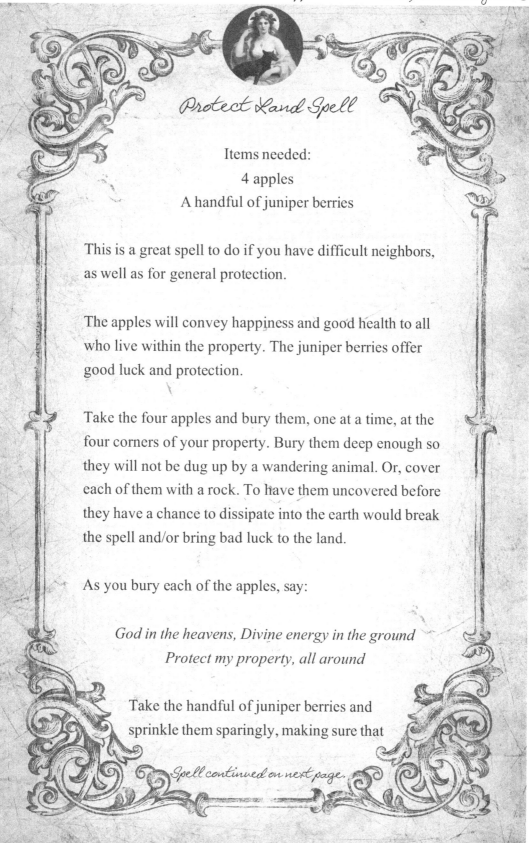

Protect Land Spell

Items needed:
4 apples
A handful of juniper berries

This is a great spell to do if you have difficult neighbors, as well as for general protection.

The apples will convey happiness and good health to all who live within the property. The juniper berries offer good luck and protection.

Take the four apples and bury them, one at a time, at the four corners of your property. Bury them deep enough so they will not be dug up by a wandering animal. Or, cover each of them with a rock. To have them uncovered before they have a chance to dissipate into the earth would break the spell and/or bring bad luck to the land.

As you bury each of the apples, say:

God in the heavens, Divine energy in the ground
Protect my property, all around

Take the handful of juniper berries and sprinkle them sparingly, making sure that

Spell continued on next page.

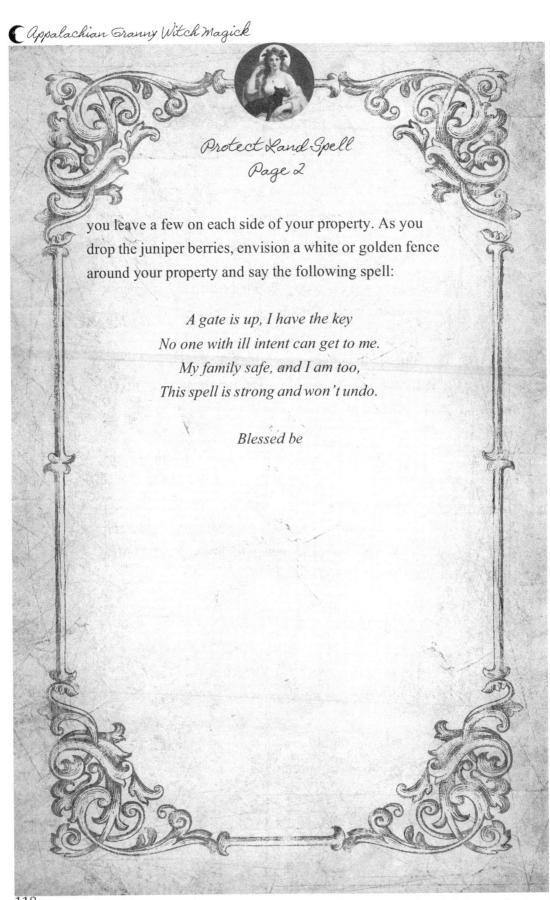

Protect Land Spell
Page 2

you leave a few on each side of your property. As you drop the juniper berries, envision a white or golden fence around your property and say the following spell:

A gate is up, I have the key
No one with ill intent can get to me.
My family safe, and I am too,
This spell is strong and won't undo.

Blessed be

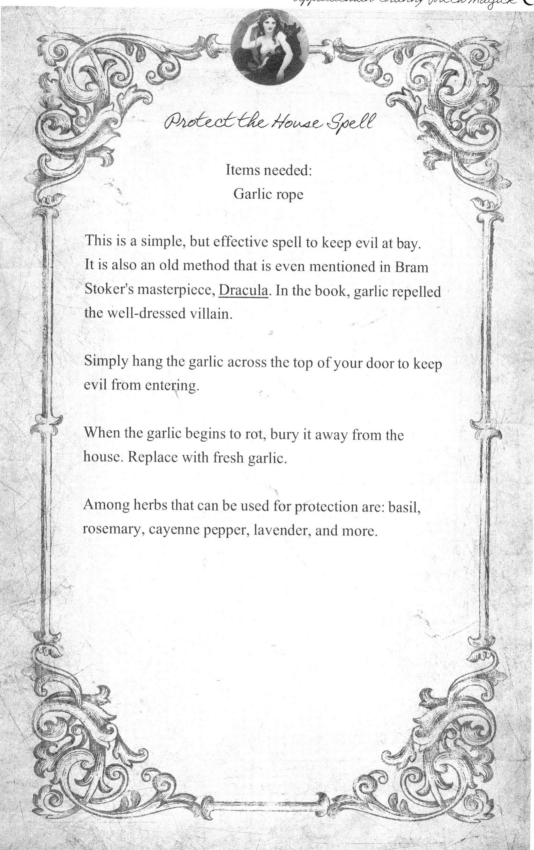

Protect the House Spell

Items needed:

Garlic rope

This is a simple, but effective spell to keep evil at bay. It is also an old method that is even mentioned in Bram Stoker's masterpiece, <u>Dracula</u>. In the book, garlic repelled the well-dressed villain.

Simply hang the garlic across the top of your door to keep evil from entering.

When the garlic begins to rot, bury it away from the house. Replace with fresh garlic.

Among herbs that can be used for protection are: basil, rosemary, cayenne pepper, lavender, and more.

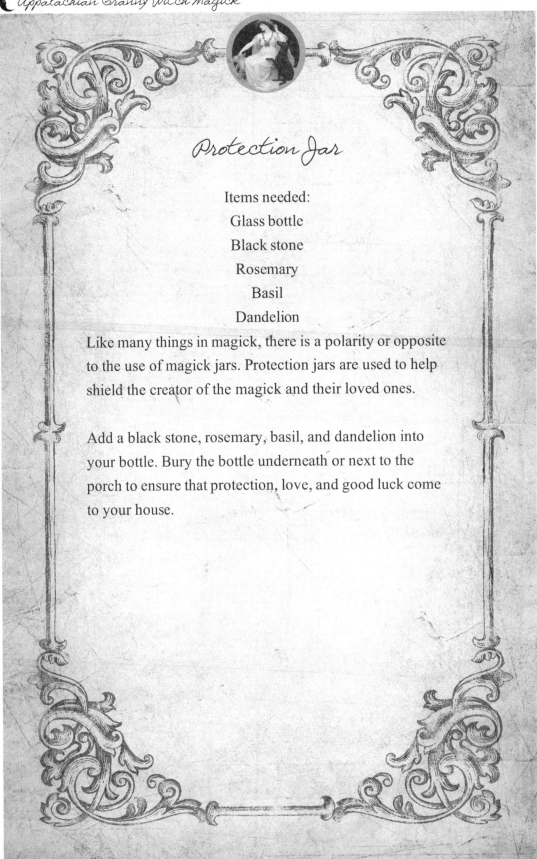

Protection Jar

Items needed:

Glass bottle

Black stone

Rosemary

Basil

Dandelion

Like many things in magick, there is a polarity or opposite to the use of magick jars. Protection jars are used to help shield the creator of the magick and their loved ones.

Add a black stone, rosemary, basil, and dandelion into your bottle. Bury the bottle underneath or next to the porch to ensure that protection, love, and good luck come to your house.

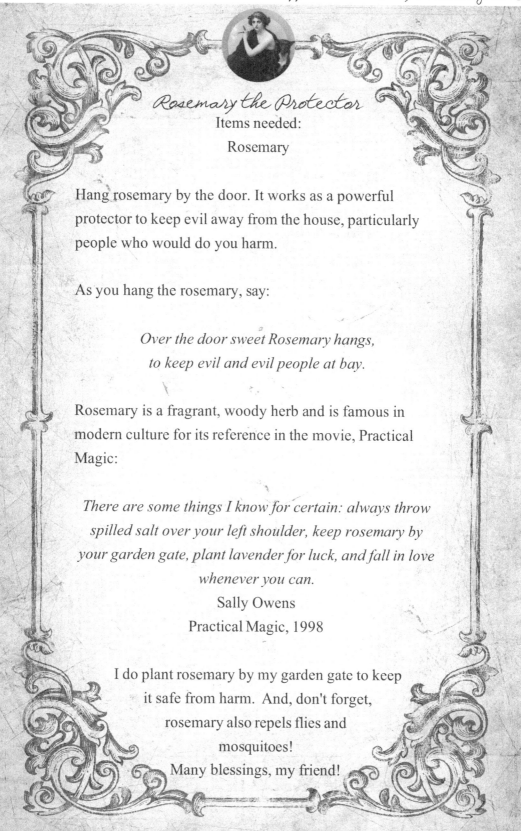

Rosemary the Protector

Items needed:

Rosemary

Hang rosemary by the door. It works as a powerful protector to keep evil away from the house, particularly people who would do you harm.

As you hang the rosemary, say:

> *Over the door sweet Rosemary hangs,*
> *to keep evil and evil people at bay.*

Rosemary is a fragrant, woody herb and is famous in modern culture for its reference in the movie, Practical Magic:

> *There are some things I know for certain: always throw*
> *spilled salt over your left shoulder, keep rosemary by*
> *your garden gate, plant lavender for luck, and fall in love*
> *whenever you can.*
> Sally Owens
> Practical Magic, 1998

I do plant rosemary by my garden gate to keep it safe from harm. And, don't forget, rosemary also repels flies and mosquitoes!
Many blessings, my friend!

Tell the Truth Spell

Items needed:
Peppermint & Lemon Balm Tea
Sandalwood Incense

Prepare a tea of peppermint and lemon balm. Light an incense stick of sandalwood. Give the tea to the person whose truth you doubt. Allow them to enjoy the tea, while making sure the sandalwood incense is permeating the air.

Then, say the following spell under your breath:

Lies on the lips, too easy to do.
Truth on the lips will stick like glue.

The person who drank the tea will begin to speak the truth after the spell.

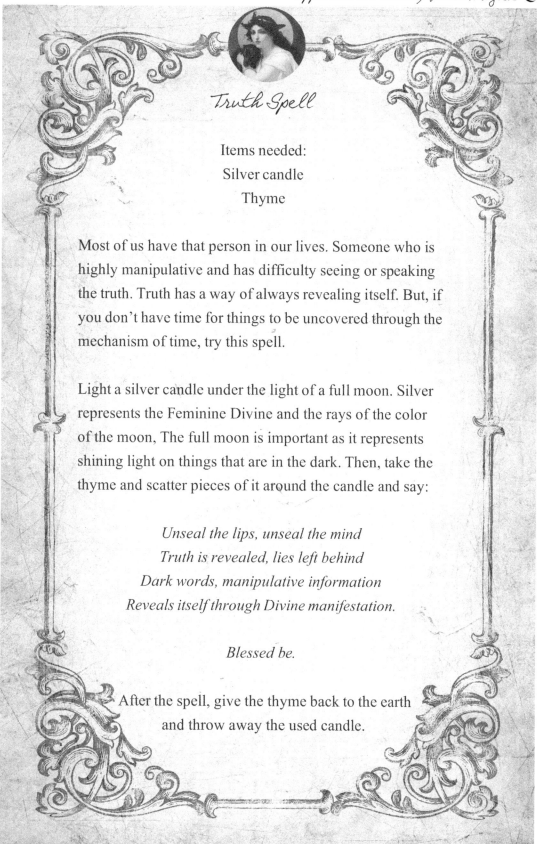

Truth Spell

Items needed:
Silver candle
Thyme

Most of us have that person in our lives. Someone who is highly manipulative and has difficulty seeing or speaking the truth. Truth has a way of always revealing itself. But, if you don't have time for things to be uncovered through the mechanism of time, try this spell.

Light a silver candle under the light of a full moon. Silver represents the Feminine Divine and the rays of the color of the moon, The full moon is important as it represents shining light on things that are in the dark. Then, take the thyme and scatter pieces of it around the candle and say:

Unseal the lips, unseal the mind
Truth is revealed, lies left behind
Dark words, manipulative information
Reveals itself through Divine manifestation.

Blessed be.

After the spell, give the thyme back to the earth and throw away the used candle.

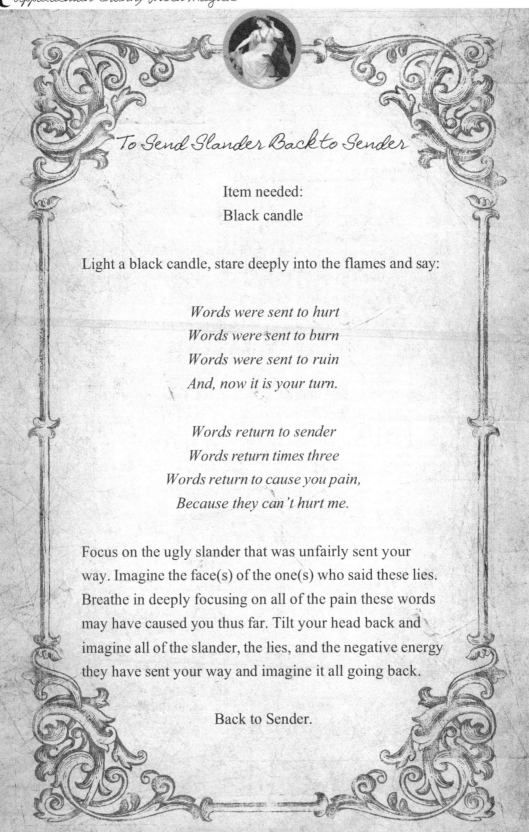

To Send Slander Back to Sender

Item needed:
Black candle

Light a black candle, stare deeply into the flames and say:

> *Words were sent to hurt*
> *Words were sent to burn*
> *Words were sent to ruin*
> *And, now it is your turn.*

> *Words return to sender*
> *Words return times three*
> *Words return to cause you pain,*
> *Because they can't hurt me.*

Focus on the ugly slander that was unfairly sent your way. Imagine the face(s) of the one(s) who said these lies. Breathe in deeply focusing on all of the pain these words may have caused you thus far. Tilt your head back and imagine all of the slander, the lies, and the negative energy they have sent your way and imagine it all going back.

Back to Sender.

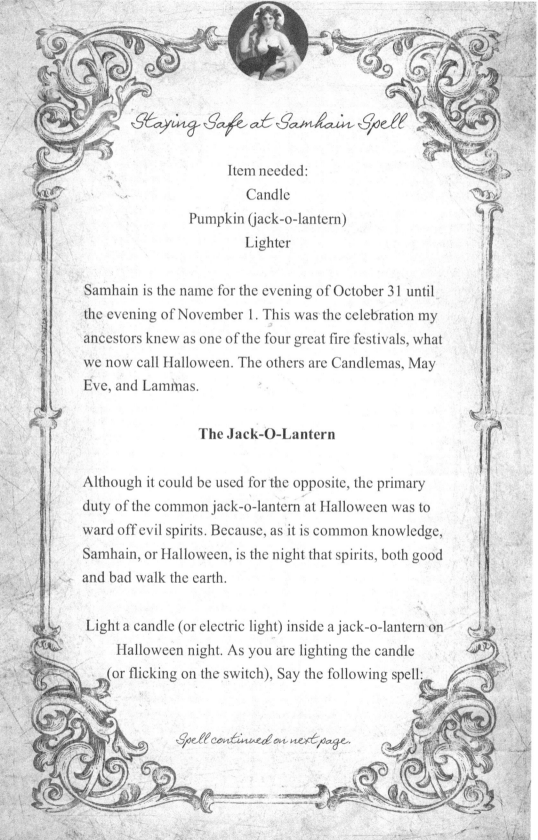

Staying Safe at Samhain Spell

Item needed:

Candle

Pumpkin (jack-o-lantern)

Lighter

Samhain is the name for the evening of October 31 until the evening of November 1. This was the celebration my ancestors knew as one of the four great fire festivals, what we now call Halloween. The others are Candlemas, May Eve, and Lammas.

The Jack-O-Lantern

Although it could be used for the opposite, the primary duty of the common jack-o-lantern at Halloween was to ward off evil spirits. Because, as it is common knowledge, Samhain, or Halloween, is the night that spirits, both good and bad walk the earth.

Light a candle (or electric light) inside a jack-o-lantern on Halloween night. As you are lighting the candle (or flicking on the switch), Say the following spell:

Spell continued on next page.

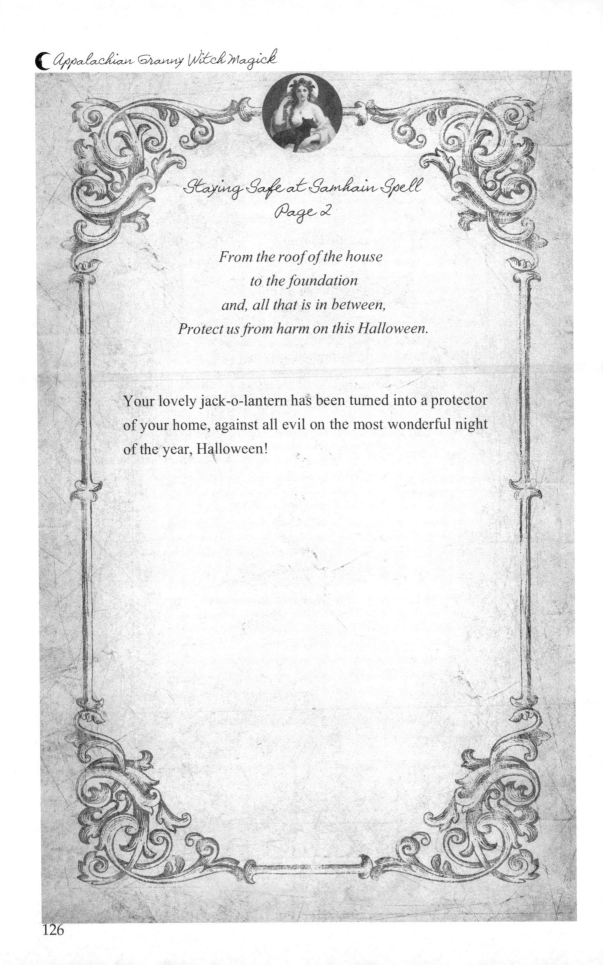

Staying Safe at Samhain Spell
Page 2

From the roof of the house
to the foundation
and, all that is in between,
Protect us from harm on this Halloween.

Your lovely jack-o-lantern has been turned into a protector of your home, against all evil on the most wonderful night of the year, Halloween!

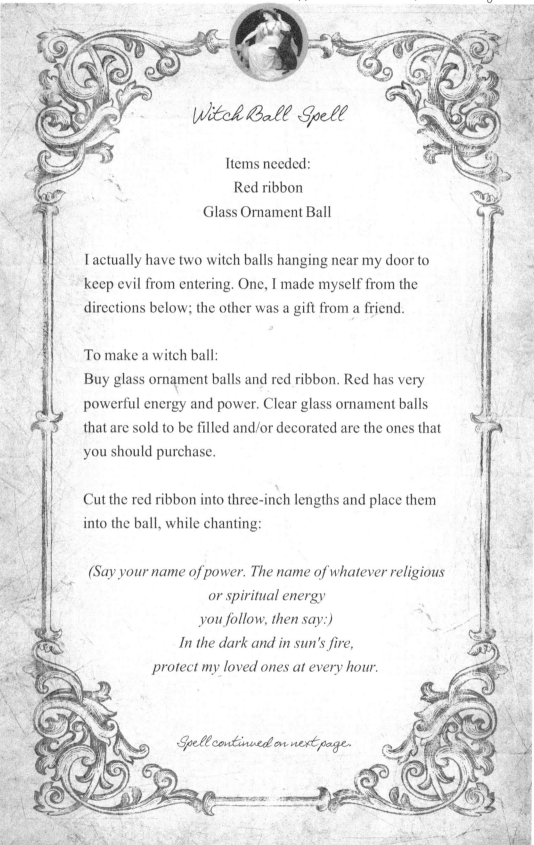

Witch Ball Spell

Items needed:
Red ribbon
Glass Ornament Ball

I actually have two witch balls hanging near my door to keep evil from entering. One, I made myself from the directions below; the other was a gift from a friend.

To make a witch ball:
Buy glass ornament balls and red ribbon. Red has very powerful energy and power. Clear glass ornament balls that are sold to be filled and/or decorated are the ones that you should purchase.

Cut the red ribbon into three-inch lengths and place them into the ball, while chanting:

(Say your name of power. The name of whatever religious
or spiritual energy
you follow, then say:)
In the dark and in sun's fire,
protect my loved ones at every hour.

Spell continued on next page.

Witch Ball Spell
Page 2

When the witch ball is full of cut, red ribbons, then hang it near the door for protection. Make sure that the witch ball is hanging in a way that it is free to turn.

I've heard it said that if evil is coming, the witch ball will begin to turn. It is a way of announcing negative energy at the same time it is working to repel that energy from your doorstep.

There are many ways to make a witch ball, but I am drawn to this version.

Self Care
Spells

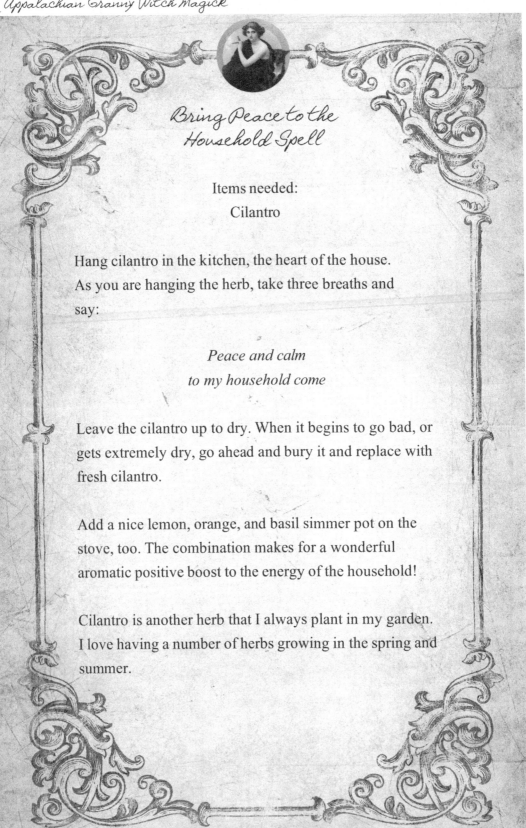

Bring Peace to the Household Spell

Items needed:

Cilantro

Hang cilantro in the kitchen, the heart of the house. As you are hanging the herb, take three breaths and say:

Peace and calm
to my household come

Leave the cilantro up to dry. When it begins to go bad, or gets extremely dry, go ahead and bury it and replace with fresh cilantro.

Add a nice lemon, orange, and basil simmer pot on the stove, too. The combination makes for a wonderful aromatic positive boost to the energy of the household!

Cilantro is another herb that I always plant in my garden. I love having a number of herbs growing in the spring and summer.

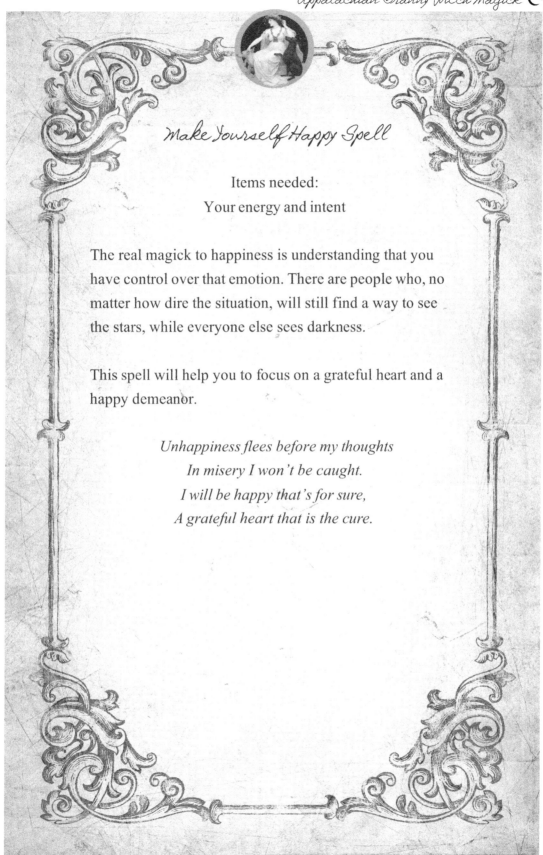

Make Yourself Happy Spell

Items needed:

Your energy and intent

The real magick to happiness is understanding that you have control over that emotion. There are people who, no matter how dire the situation, will still find a way to see the stars, while everyone else sees darkness.

This spell will help you to focus on a grateful heart and a happy demeanor.

Unhappiness flees before my thoughts
In misery I won't be caught.
I will be happy that's for sure,
A grateful heart that is the cure.

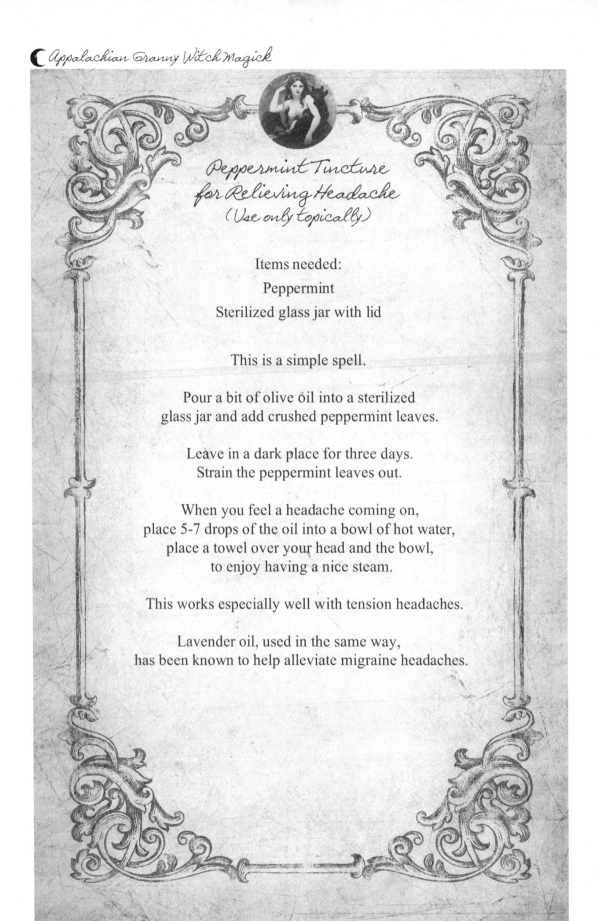

Peppermint Tincture for Relieving Headache
(Use only topically)

Items needed:

Peppermint

Sterilized glass jar with lid

This is a simple spell.

Pour a bit of olive oil into a sterilized
glass jar and add crushed peppermint leaves.

Leave in a dark place for three days.
Strain the peppermint leaves out.

When you feel a headache coming on,
place 5-7 drops of the oil into a bowl of hot water,
place a towel over your head and the bowl,
to enjoy having a nice steam.

This works especially well with tension headaches.

Lavender oil, used in the same way,
has been known to help alleviate migraine headaches.

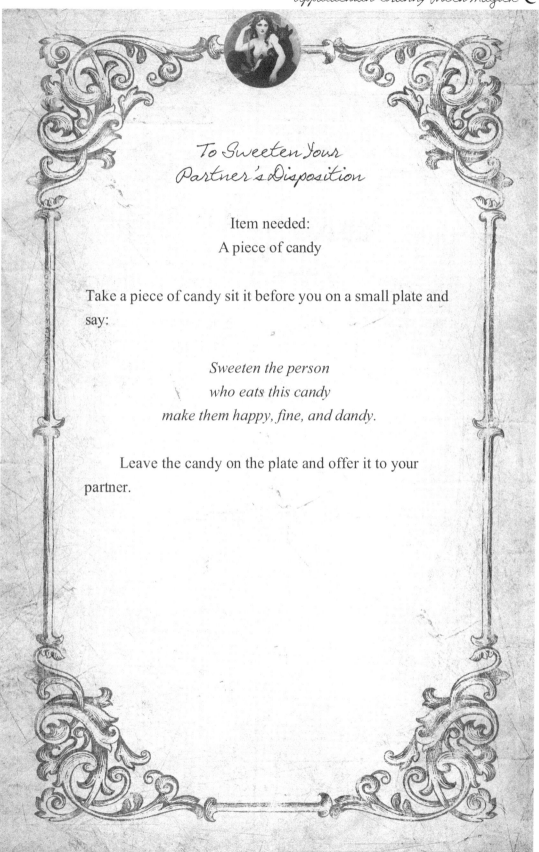

To Sweeten Your Partner's Disposition

Item needed:
A piece of candy

Take a piece of candy sit it before you on a small plate and say:

Sweeten the person
who eats this candy
make them happy, fine, and dandy.

Leave the candy on the plate and offer it to your partner.

Wax Ball Spell to Bring Happiness

Items needed:
Wax (preferably beeswax)
Small Pieces of citrine
Lemon balm

Melt the wax, then place the citrine and lemon balm into the container with the melted wax. Think pleasant and positive thoughts as you create the wax ball.

Leave the wax to begin to harden. While it is still soft, but cool enough to work with, take the wax and roll it into a ball.

Roll the wax ball across the doorstep of the front door to bring happiness into your home.

Leave the wax ball next to your door for three days and three nights. At the end of that time, bury the wax ball under a healthy tree. As the tree grows, your happiness will too.

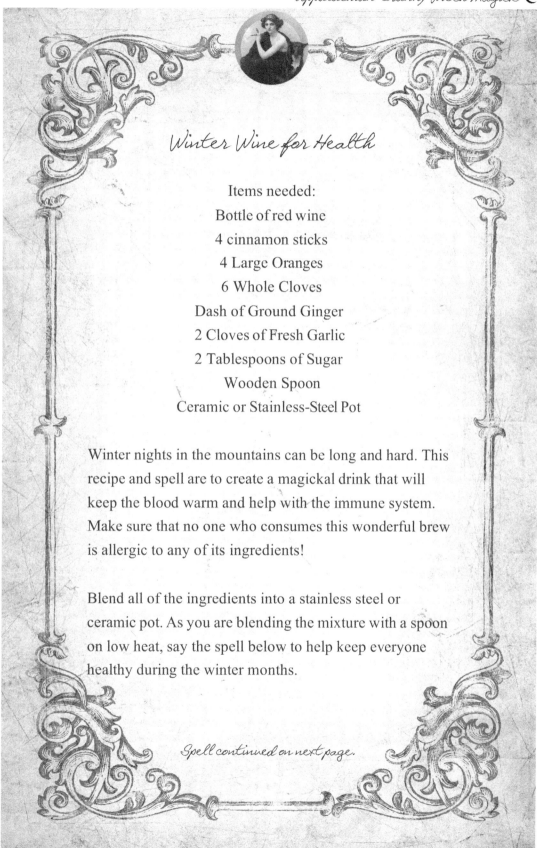

Winter Wine for Health

Items needed:
Bottle of red wine
4 cinnamon sticks
4 Large Oranges
6 Whole Cloves
Dash of Ground Ginger
2 Cloves of Fresh Garlic
2 Tablespoons of Sugar
Wooden Spoon
Ceramic or Stainless-Steel Pot

Winter nights in the mountains can be long and hard. This recipe and spell are to create a magickal drink that will keep the blood warm and help with the immune system. Make sure that no one who consumes this wonderful brew is allergic to any of its ingredients!

Blend all of the ingredients into a stainless steel or ceramic pot. As you are blending the mixture with a spoon on low heat, say the spell below to help keep everyone healthy during the winter months.

Spell continued on next page.

Winter Wine for Health
Page 2

With each stir of the spoon,
With each cup of wine that is consumed,
My loved ones will become immune,
To sickness great and small.

Bring the heat up to medium, but make sure the wine never boils.

Let the wine and mixture simmer for 20 minutes. Strain while still warm.

As you pour a cup for you and whoever else, focus on the wine and all of the health it will give to your loved ones.

Spells to
Bring Sleep +
Prevent Nightmares

Spells to Bring Sleep and Prevent Nightmares

To Soothe Thoughts

Items needed:

Rosemary sprigs

Cord

Wrap the ends of some rosemary sprigs and hang them above your bed.

Dream Pillow

Items needed:

Lavender

Pillow

Place some lavender inside your pillowcase, the opposite side from where you lay your head.

Magickal Teas for Sleep

Items needed:

Valerian tea

Chamomile tea

Lavender tea

Drink a lovely cup of Valerian root tea, when you have a particularly bad time trying to sleep.

Spell continued on next page.

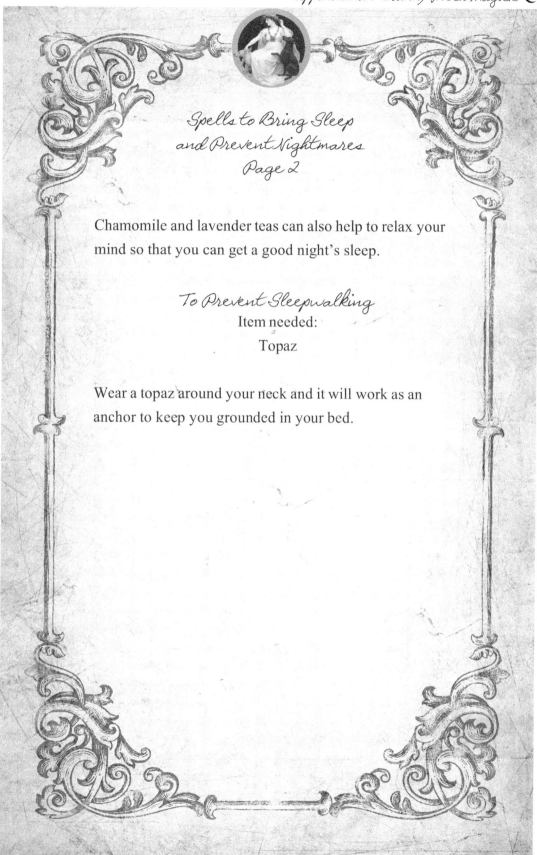

Spells to Bring Sleep and Prevent Nightmares
Page 2

Chamomile and lavender teas can also help to relax your mind so that you can get a good night's sleep.

To Prevent Sleepwalking
Item needed:
Topaz

Wear a topaz around your neck and it will work as an anchor to keep you grounded in your bed.

Wishing
Spells

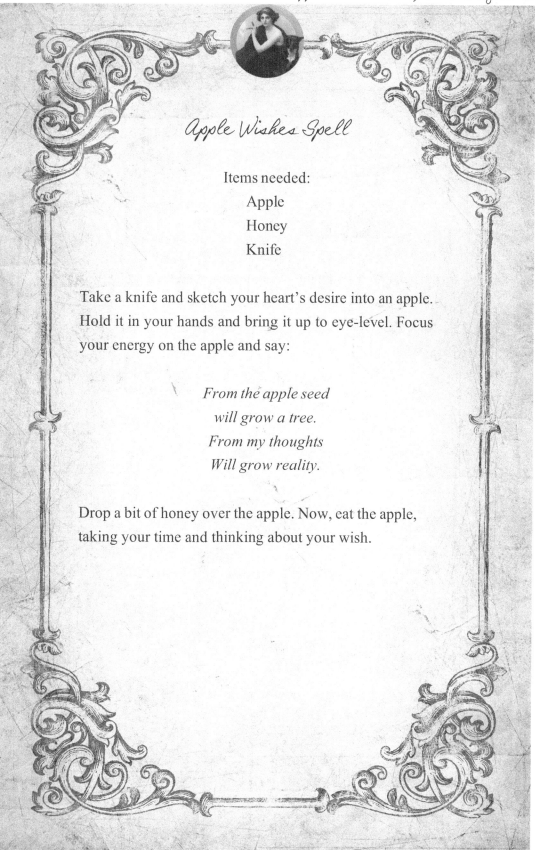

Apple Wishes Spell

Items needed:
Apple
Honey
Knife

Take a knife and sketch your heart's desire into an apple. Hold it in your hands and bring it up to eye-level. Focus your energy on the apple and say:

From the apple seed
will grow a tree.
From my thoughts
Will grow reality.

Drop a bit of honey over the apple. Now, eat the apple, taking your time and thinking about your wish.

Dandelion Wishes

Item needed:
Dandelion

This is a beautiful spell that is done by children everywhere this amazing plant grows, including the Appalachian Mountains. Pick a dandelion from the yard. Think about what you would like to manifest in your life. Take a deep breath and blow all of the seeds off of the dandelion at once, watching them as they are carried by the wind.

Your wish should come true.

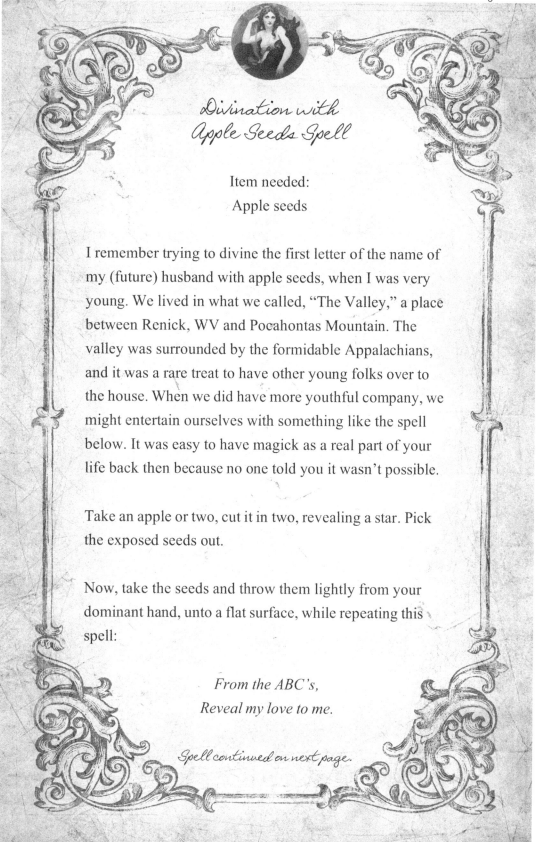

Divination with Apple Seeds Spell

Item needed:
Apple seeds

I remember trying to divine the first letter of the name of my (future) husband with apple seeds, when I was very young. We lived in what we called, "The Valley," a place between Renick, WV and Pocahontas Mountain. The valley was surrounded by the formidable Appalachians, and it was a rare treat to have other young folks over to the house. When we did have more youthful company, we might entertain ourselves with something like the spell below. It was easy to have magick as a real part of your life back then because no one told you it wasn't possible.

Take an apple or two, cut it in two, revealing a star. Pick the exposed seeds out.

Now, take the seeds and throw them lightly from your dominant hand, unto a flat surface, while repeating this spell:

From the ABC's,
Reveal my love to me.

Spell continued on next page.

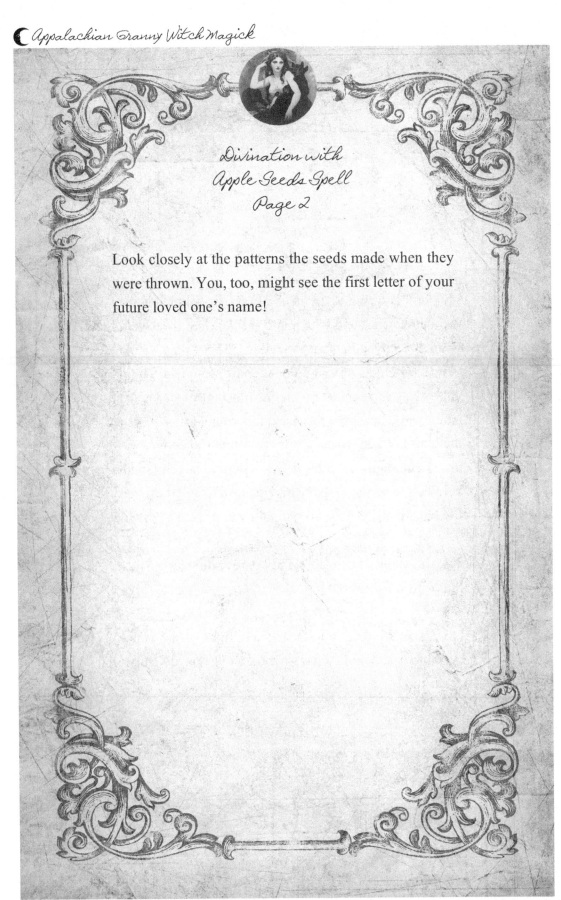

*Divination with
Apple Seeds Spell
Page 2*

Look closely at the patterns the seeds made when they were thrown. You, too, might see the first letter of your future loved one's name!

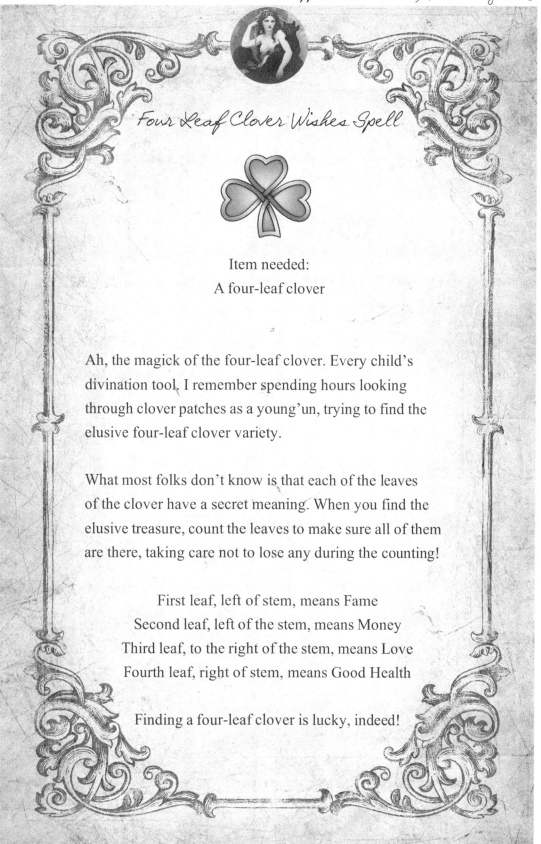

Four Leaf Clover Wishes Spell

Item needed:
A four-leaf clover

Ah, the magick of the four-leaf clover. Every child's divination tool. I remember spending hours looking through clover patches as a young'un, trying to find the elusive four-leaf clover variety.

What most folks don't know is that each of the leaves of the clover have a secret meaning. When you find the elusive treasure, count the leaves to make sure all of them are there, taking care not to lose any during the counting!

First leaf, left of stem, means Fame
Second leaf, left of the stem, means Money
Third leaf, to the right of the stem, means Love
Fourth leaf, right of stem, means Good Health

Finding a four-leaf clover is lucky, indeed!

Sundry
Spells

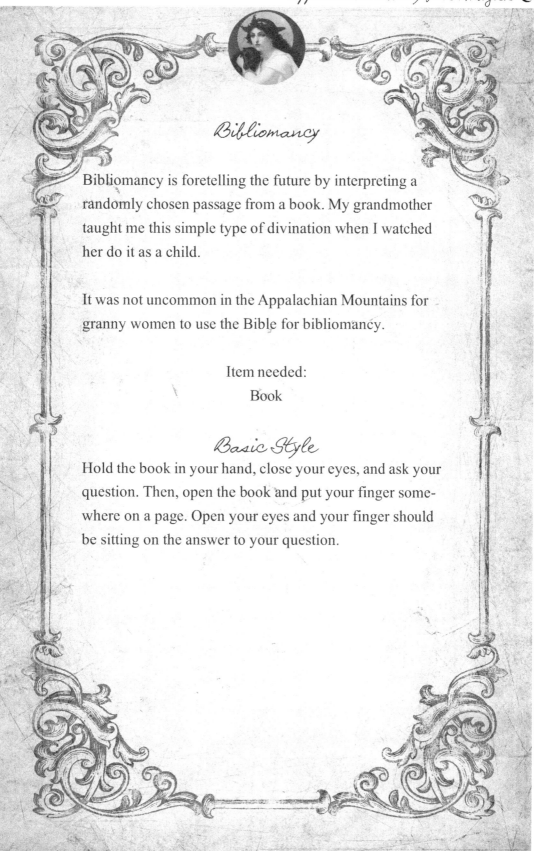

Bibliomancy

Bibliomancy is foretelling the future by interpreting a randomly chosen passage from a book. My grandmother taught me this simple type of divination when I watched her do it as a child.

It was not uncommon in the Appalachian Mountains for granny women to use the Bible for bibliomancy.

Item needed:
Book

Basic Style

Hold the book in your hand, close your eyes, and ask your question. Then, open the book and put your finger somewhere on a page. Open your eyes and your finger should be sitting on the answer to your question.

Bibliomancy Pinpoint Accuracy

Item needed:

Book

Pin

Before beginning the bibliomancy session, say this short spell:

Within this book my answer lies.
And, I will find the answer wise.

Place the book on a flat table, put the pin in your dominant hand, close your eyes, and ask your question. Open the book and bring your hand down with the pin somewhere on a page, make sure that you skewer the pin through the page. Open your eyes and the pin will have marked the passage in the book that is the answer to your question.

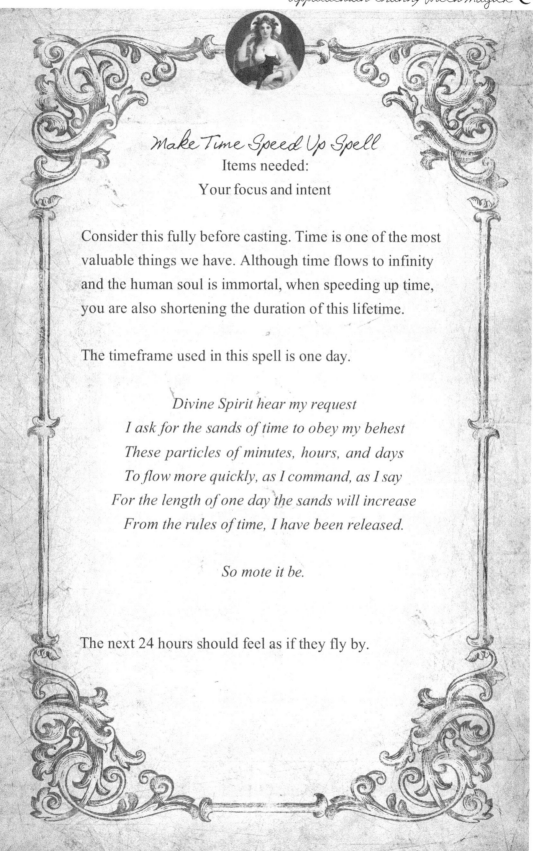

Make Time Speed Up Spell

Items needed:

Your focus and intent

Consider this fully before casting. Time is one of the most valuable things we have. Although time flows to infinity and the human soul is immortal, when speeding up time, you are also shortening the duration of this lifetime.

The timeframe used in this spell is one day.

Divine Spirit hear my request
I ask for the sands of time to obey my behest
These particles of minutes, hours, and days
To flow more quickly, as I command, as I say
For the length of one day the sands will increase
From the rules of time, I have been released.

So mote it be.

The next 24 hours should feel as if they fly by.

Phoenix Transformation in the Dream State Spell

Items needed:
Frankincense
Meditation music

The immortal phoenix is inevitably consumed by its own fire, but is then reborn, time and time again. In this spell, you will be reborn into the astral plane in the form of the phoenix, to live the night as the ageless legend. To soar to heights within the astral realm that you have not climbed to before. To transform into a phoenix in the dream state to move through the astral plane in that form, do the following spell.

Place meditation music on as you are preparing for bed. Light some Frankincense incense near the bed, but in a very safe container, away from anything that might catch on fire. Say the following spell:

Spell continued on next page.

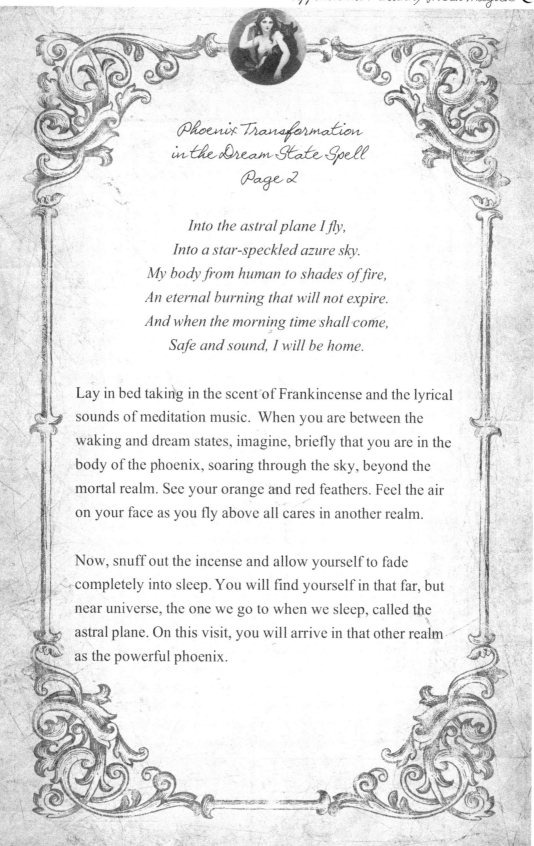

Phoenix Transformation in the Dream State Spell
Page 2

Into the astral plane I fly,
Into a star-speckled azure sky.
My body from human to shades of fire,
An eternal burning that will not expire.
And when the morning time shall come,
Safe and sound, I will be home.

Lay in bed taking in the scent of Frankincense and the lyrical sounds of meditation music. When you are between the waking and dream states, imagine, briefly that you are in the body of the phoenix, soaring through the sky, beyond the mortal realm. See your orange and red feathers. Feel the air on your face as you fly above all cares in another realm.

Now, snuff out the incense and allow yourself to fade completely into sleep. You will find yourself in that far, but near universe, the one we go to when we sleep, called the astral plane. On this visit, you will arrive in that other realm as the powerful phoenix.

Chapter 10

Musings on Future Generations

d. Sunflower.   e. Fig-Marygold.

For most of us, the only immortality we will know from this lifetime is that which is carried through our bloodlines. We, ourselves, have an immortal energy that will move on, hopefully, to rejoin those we knew and loved during this lifetime. But we move on in spirit to another time and another place, leaving these moments in time behind.

Children and grandchildren provide that link between this life and our immortal spirits. They carry on our DNA and will transfer our and other ancestors' genetic memories to our lineage until we are reborn at some point.

In my case, I have the pleasure of being a granny to Anna, a little dynamo of energy that has given me more joy than I can express! Since she was a baby, I shared stories of magick with her. Faeries, trolls, elves, and more elementals were part of the literary landscape that I ushered her through.

The beautiful energy of these stories transferred into our world, as we created a special place known as the "faerie tree." We've hung sparkly suncatchers in the tree, as it's known that the faeries love anything, but coins, which are shiny! We've also hung a birdhouse so that it would attract small birds. The Fae are known to use our feathered friends as transportation.

For the last few springs and summers, Anna and I have sat under this tree, overlooking the Blue Ridge Mountains. Reading stories, talking, and sometimes just sitting in silence, enjoying the view of the magnificent mountains.

My greatest wish is that Anna remembers these talks and the faeries when I am gone. That she will look for magick, because it is all around us. And, that she will remember how much I loved her and how special to me those hours with her were.

I am so blessed to have my daughters Megan and Stephanie and their husbands, in my life. They have been my world. Megan is earning her Master's degree and living in Italy as I write, and I could not be more proud of her. Stephanie is the mother of Anna and of the plethora of horses and other animals on her and her husband's farm. She is an amazing person in her own right.

The psychic gifts that I have were handed down to Anna. When she was four, I bought her a small vintage chair, which her mom put in her bedroom. One night, Stephanie woke up to Anna standing next to the bed. "Mommy," she said, "can I sleep with you? That little girl on the chair won't quit staring at me."

She also has a witchy spark in her. On the next page are Anna's first two spells. We worked on them together, but she was adamant as to what they were to be about. The first is how to turn cake into a bird. And the second is how to make a traffic light change. The imagination of a child is, in itself, magickal!

Anna's First Spells

Cake to Birds Spell

Little bird, eat this cake,

then little baby birds you'll make.

Lights Spell

Stop or go, red or green,

take heed,

the light will change to meet my needs.

Anna's first spell, age 5.

Most of us have heard the expression, "They don't stay little forever," and it is so true. As parents and grandparents, we can help build a foundation upon which a child can travel through the power of their imagination to any destination and do anything to which they set their mind, heart, and ambition. Such is the essence of true magick.

The children of this region have so much to be proud of; they are the sons and daughters of the mountains upon which the granny women and conjure men lived their lives. There is no better place for an Appalachian to build a life than among the mountains our ancestors called home.

Epilogue

It was a joy to write this book. A manuscript full of memories, musings, and magick. I hope you enjoyed reading it, as much as I did writing the book, Our mountain granny stories are a treasure and I have a passion for preserving at least some of them.

This passion is the inspiration for my next project, a documentary about Appalachian Granny women titled, ***There's Magick in Them Mountains***, I begin shooting the film in June of 2023. The title of the documentary is based on something that my grandmother said to me once. A poem about that moment is shared on page 5 of this book. I hope to have the documentary completed by August of 2025.

As I am an independent filmmaker, I'll be wearing many hats during this production. I am thrilled about the topic and about the challenge of making a showcase film about the granny women of the Appalachian Mountains.

I have already spoken to a number of folks who have personal stories of these amazing mountain women, and I will do all I can to preserve those stories on film for both the present and future generations.

Bibliography

Alexa. "*Being Buried Alive Was so Common in the Victorian Era That Doctors Used These 10 Methods to Prevent It.*" History Collection, 12 Aug. 2021, historycollection.com/buried-alive-common-victorian-era-doctors-used-10-methods-prevent.

Bussard, P. (2013). Thirty True Tales of the Weird, Unusual and Macabre: From the Notebooks of the Paranormal Journalist. Reaper Publishing.

Childbirth and Babies in the 1900s. www.roadtoavonlea.com/blog-posts/childbirth-and-babies-in-the-1900s#:~:text=For%20every%201000%20live%20births%20in%201900%2C%206-9,1%20year%20%28Statistic%3A%20Center%20for%20Disease%20and%20Control%29.

Ellen Guiley, Rosemary. *Fairy Magic: All about Fairies and How to Bring Their Magic into Your Life*. Harper Collins UK, 2004. p. 1.

Harkins, Anthony, and Meredith McCarroll. Appalachian Reckoning: A Region Responds to Hillbilly Elegy. 2019.

Hektoen International. "Changes in Childbirth in the United States: 1750–1950 - Hektoen International." Hektoen International - an Online Medical Humanities Journal, 10 Dec. 2019, hekint.org/2017/01/27/changes-in-childbirth-in-the-united-states-1750-1950.

"In Rural Areas With Health Care Shortages, These Doctors Are Answering the Call."
PBS NewsHour, 9 Apr. 2021, www.pbs.org/newshour/health/rural-areas-
health-care-shortages-these-doctors-are-answering-the-call.

Jaret, Peter. "Attracting the Next Generation of Physicians to Rural Medicine."
AAMC, 29 June 2022, www.aamc.org/news-insights/attracting-next-
generation-physicians-rural-medicine#:~:text=And%20while%20
20%25%20of%20 the%20U.S.%20population%20lives,unintentional%20
injury%2C%20and%20chronic%20lung%20disease%20than%20city-dwellers.

Maykin, Melissa. "Queen Elizabeth II's Bees Informed of Her Death, as Part of
a Long-standing Beekeeping Tradition." *ABC News,* 14 Sept. 2022, www.
abc.net.au/news/2022-09-14/why-royal-beekeeper-tells-bees-queen-
died/101439526.

O'Keefe, Pat. *Graveyard Voice: Poems and Photographs from the Edge of Darkness.*
Reaper Publishing, 2017.

O'Keefe, Pat Bussard, et al. *Spells and Stories of the Sisterhood of Magick and
Wonders.* Reaper Publishing, 2022.

"Plants to Ward off Evil Spirits and Spiritual Protection." My Today's Horoscope, 6
Mar. 2023, mytodayshoroscope.com/plants-that-ward-off-evil-spirits.

Randolph, Zoë. "11 Facts About the Appalachian Mountains | Mental Floss." Mental
        Floss, 11 Aug. 2021, www.mentalfloss.com/article/649146/appalachian-
        mountains-facts.

Raymond, Chris. *13 Death and Dying Superstitions – Funeral Help Center.* 16 Nov.
        2021, www.funeralhelpcenter.com/13-death-dying-superstitions.

Richards, Jake. *Backwoods Witchcraft: Conjure & Folk Magic from Appalachia.*
        Weiser Books, 2019

Roberts, Alice. "Writings." 2003.

Stoker, Bram. *Dracula*: 1897. Hoffmann and Hoffmann, 2020.

Symbolsandsynchronicity. "Brooms Spiritual Meaning and Beliefs." *Symbols and
        Synchronicity*, Dec. 2021, symbolsandsynchronicity.com/brooms-spiritual-
        meaning-beliefs-symbolism.

Thomas, Sarah. ""*Everyday Appalachian Superstitions*." Appalachian History.Net, 12
        Oct. 2020, www.appalachianhistory.net/2020/10/everyday-appalachian-
        superstitions.html.

Wikipedia contributors. (2023). Witchcraft Acts. Wikipedia. https://en.wikipedia.org/
        wiki/Witchcraft_Acts

Thank you to these Etsy Artists:

CreativeMuseGallery

EmilyEstherDesigns

FairytaleAndFables

PrintableColors

Printseys

RomanticaArts

SharmStudio

WildWickedWonders

Author's Book of Shadows created by:

Etsy Artisan CountryPinecones

About the Author

The Appalachian Mountains were the backdrop for generations of Pat O'Keefe's family. She is a latter-day granny witch, and a renowned psychic and medium. She teaches the magickal arts, as well as psychic and mediumship classes. Pat is a Consulting Hypnotist, trained through the National Guild of Hypnotists, whose practice focuses on memory recovery/ past life regressions. Although she does intuitive energy healing, she is also a trained Reiki Master. She has traveled the country conducting seances, gallery readings, energy healing sessions, classes, and workshops on a plethora of spiritual and paranormal topics. She is the author or co-author of seven books, this is her eighth.

Made in the USA
Las Vegas, NV
08 December 2023

82328897R00090